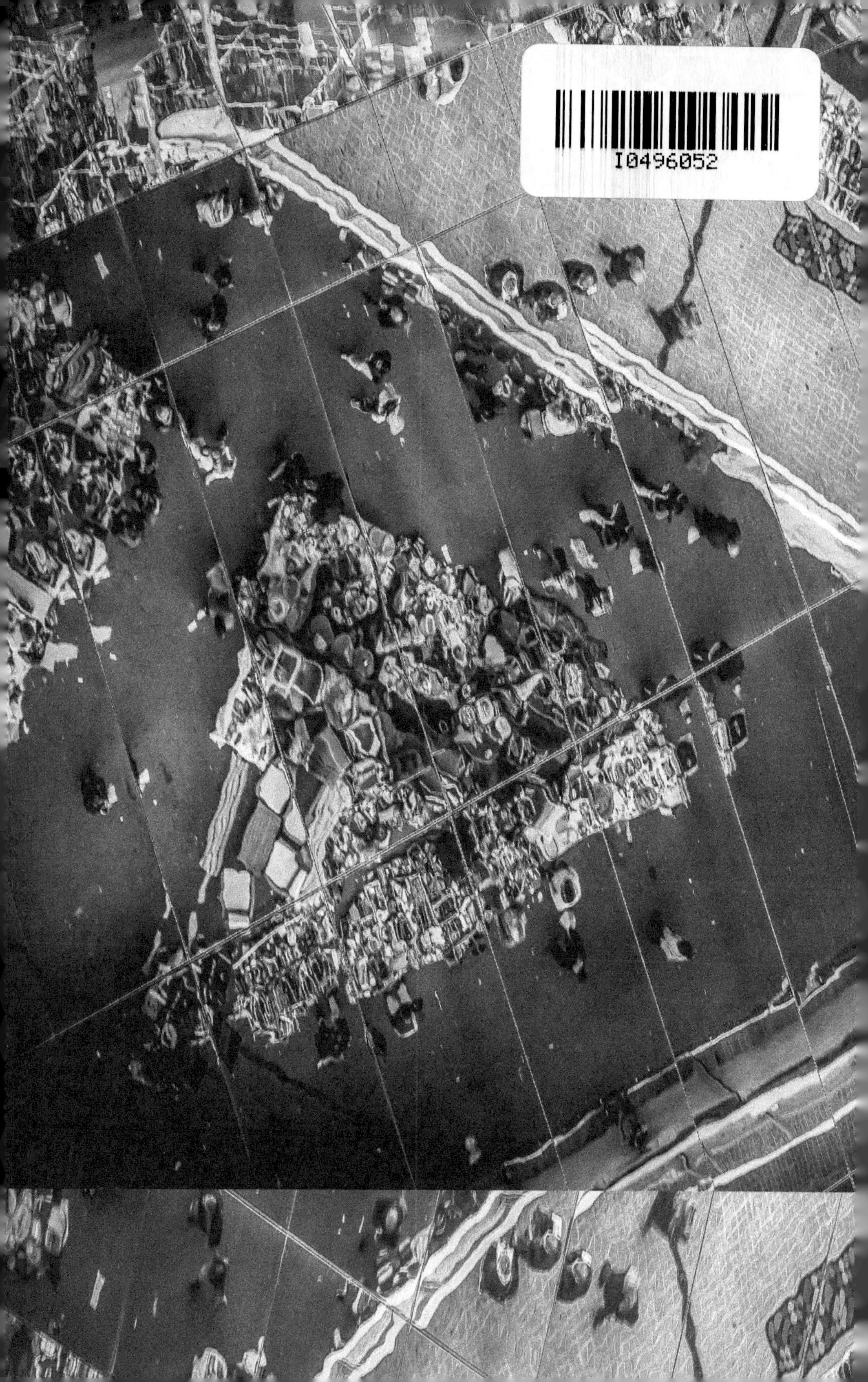

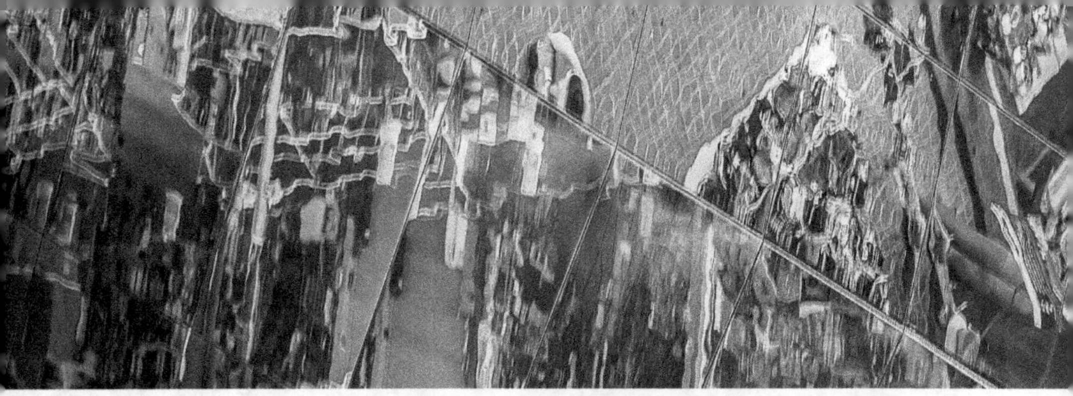

THE NEW BARCELONA
(OR NOT)

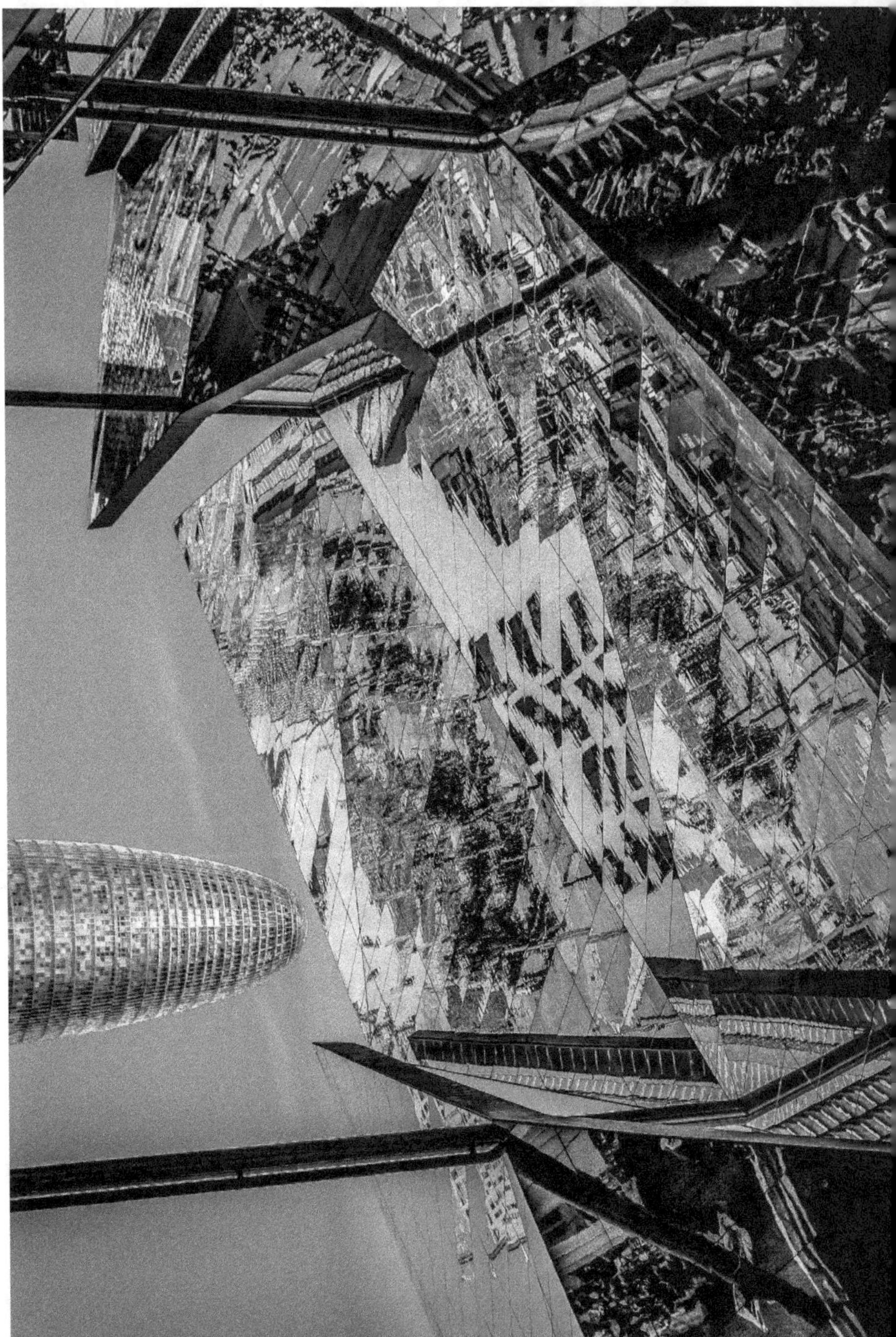

THE LAST MEN

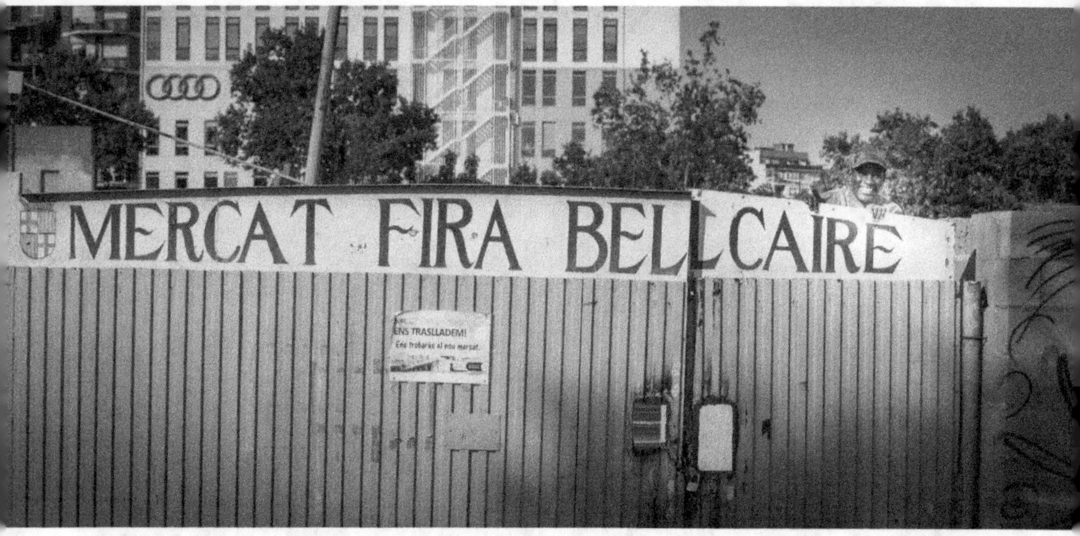
MERCAT FIRA BELLCAIRE
ENS TRASLLADEM!
Ens trobaras al nou mercat.

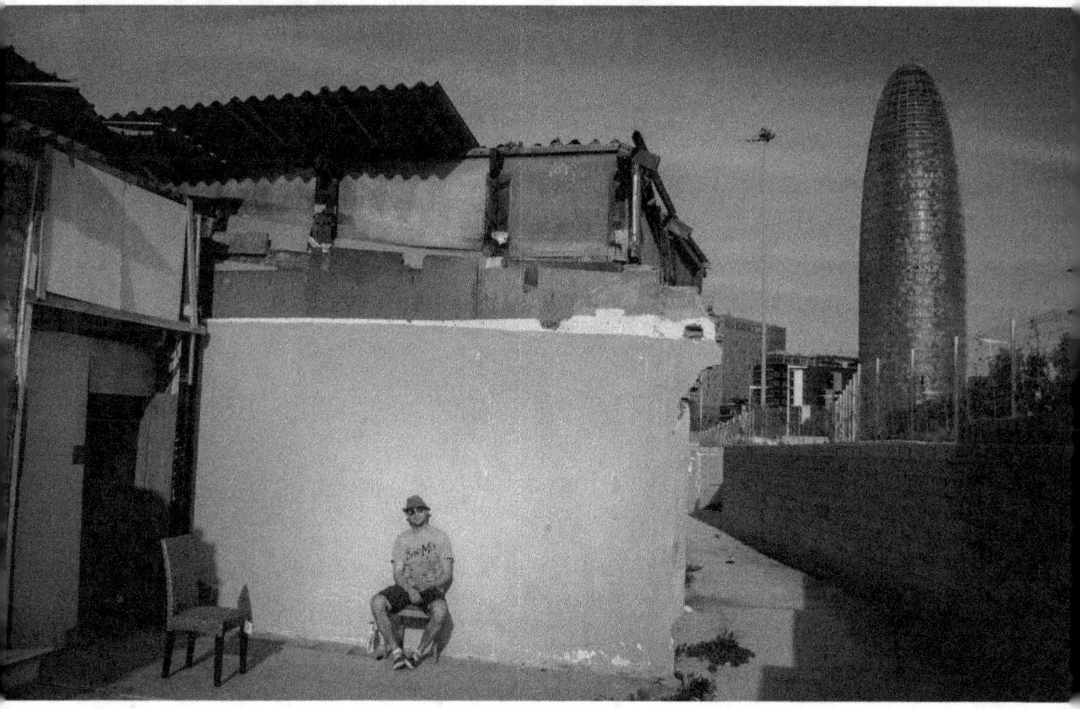

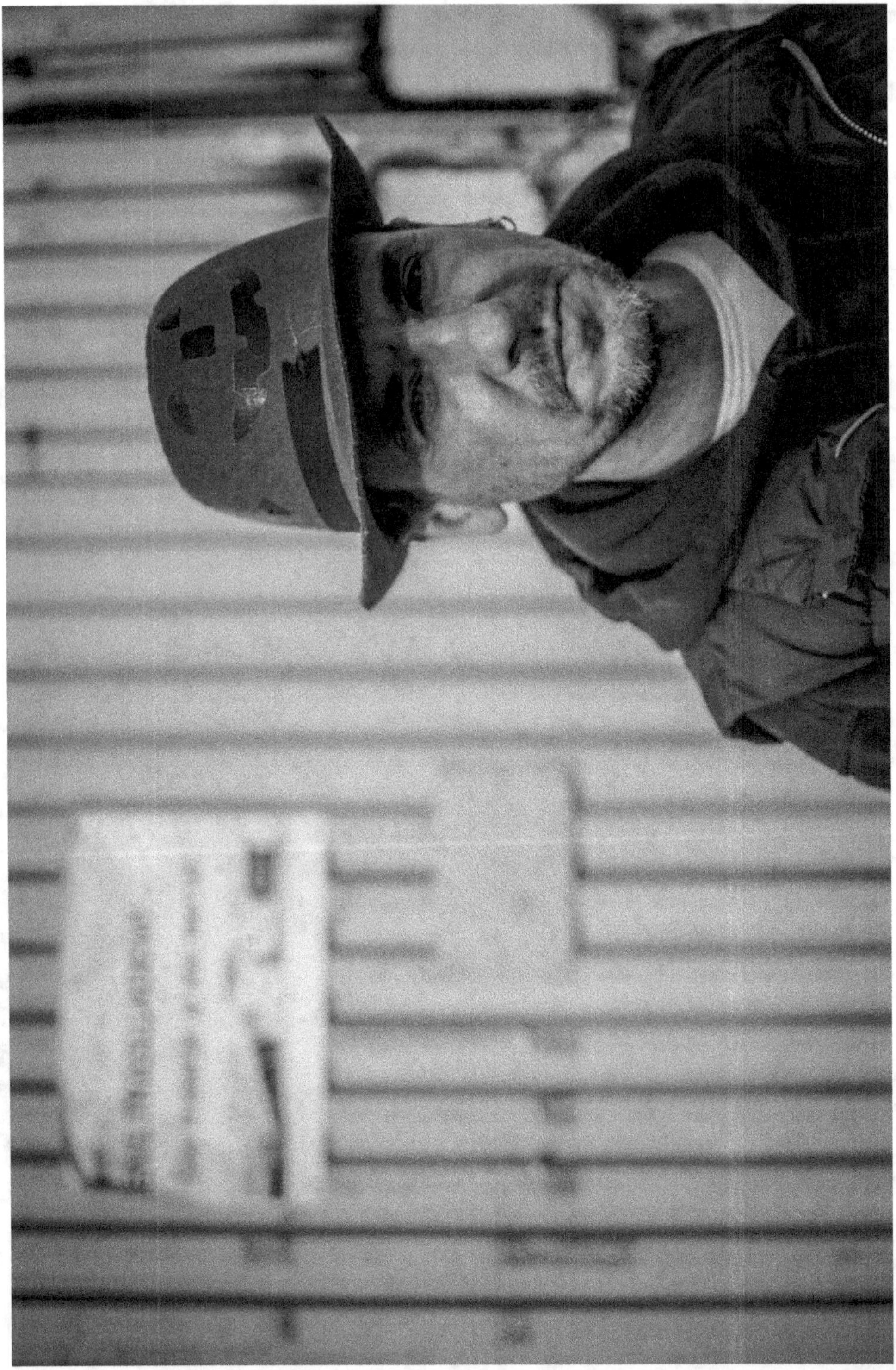

RAILWAY

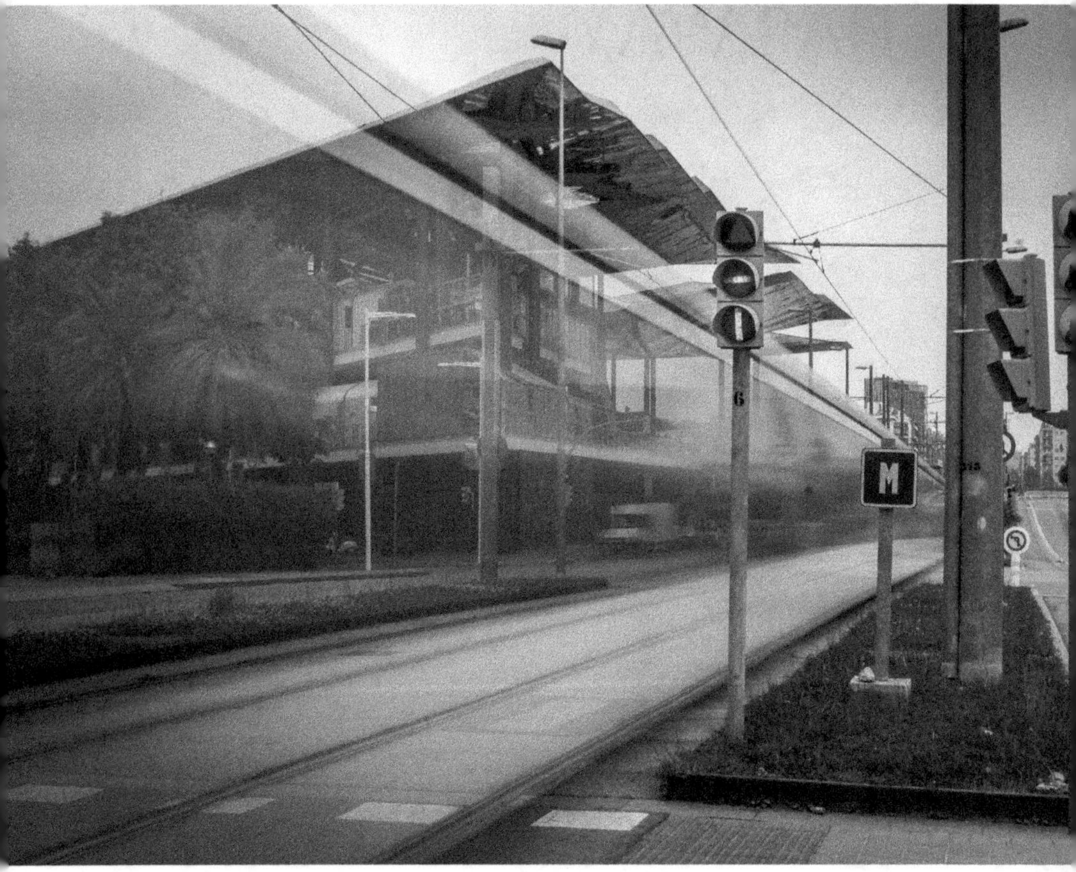
6
M

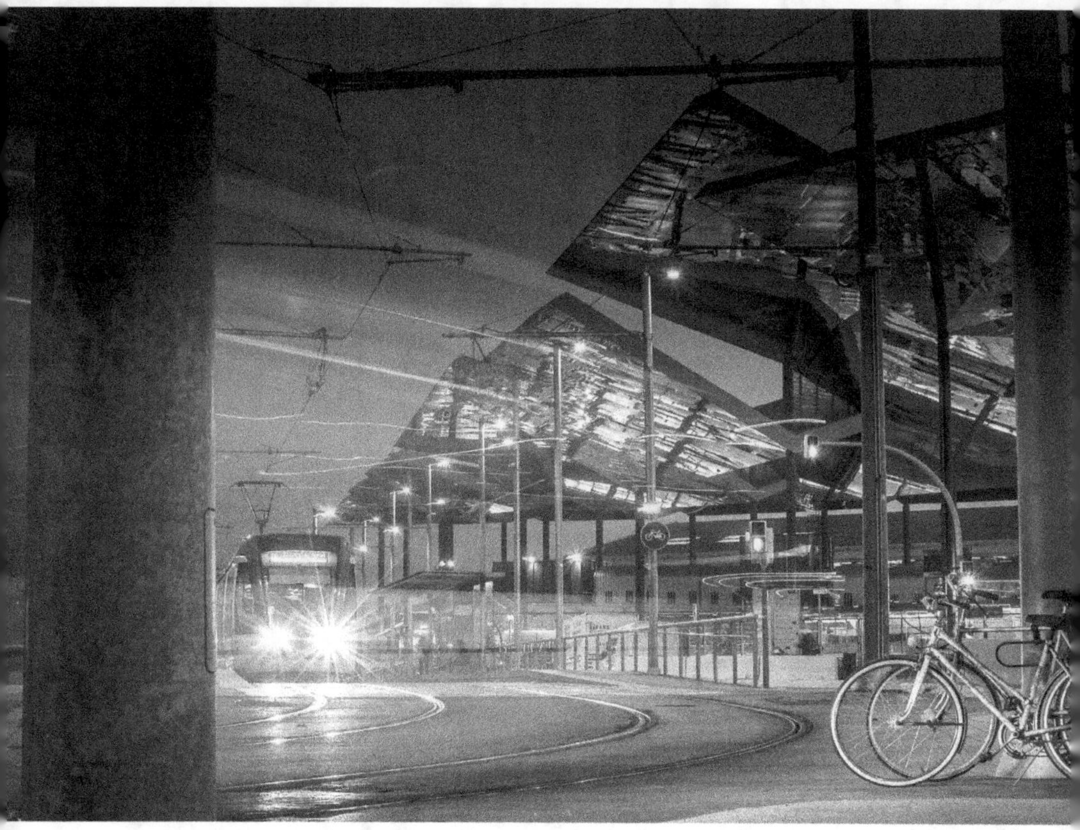

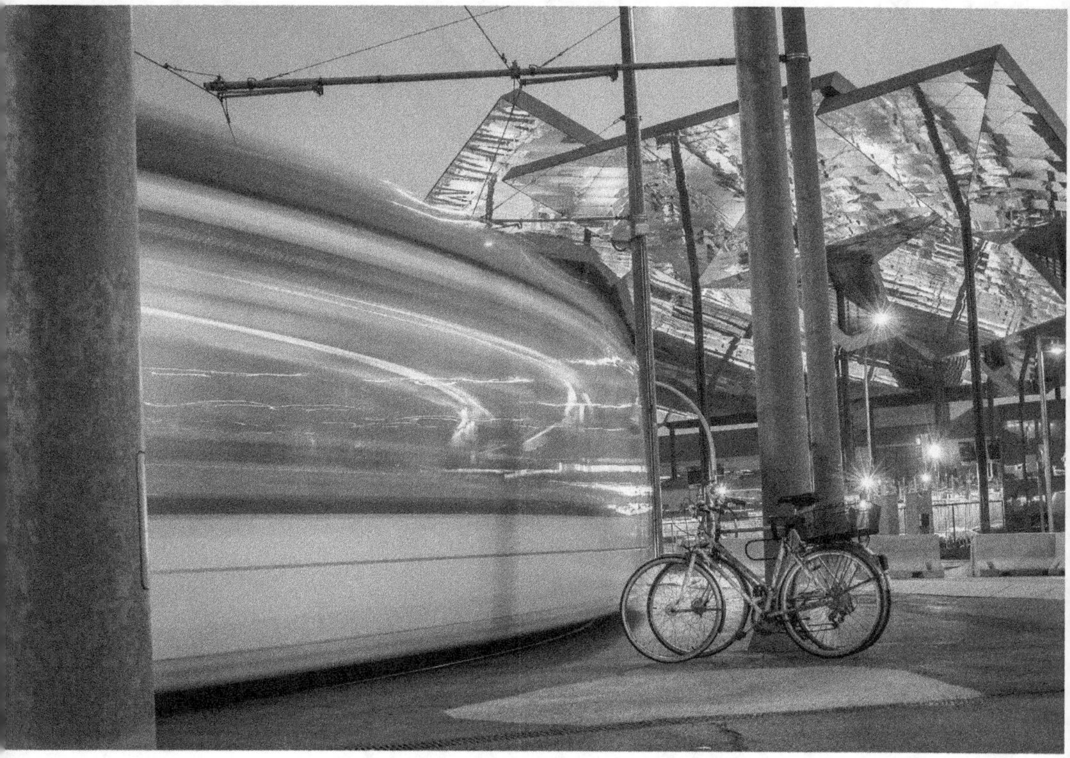

MIRRORS

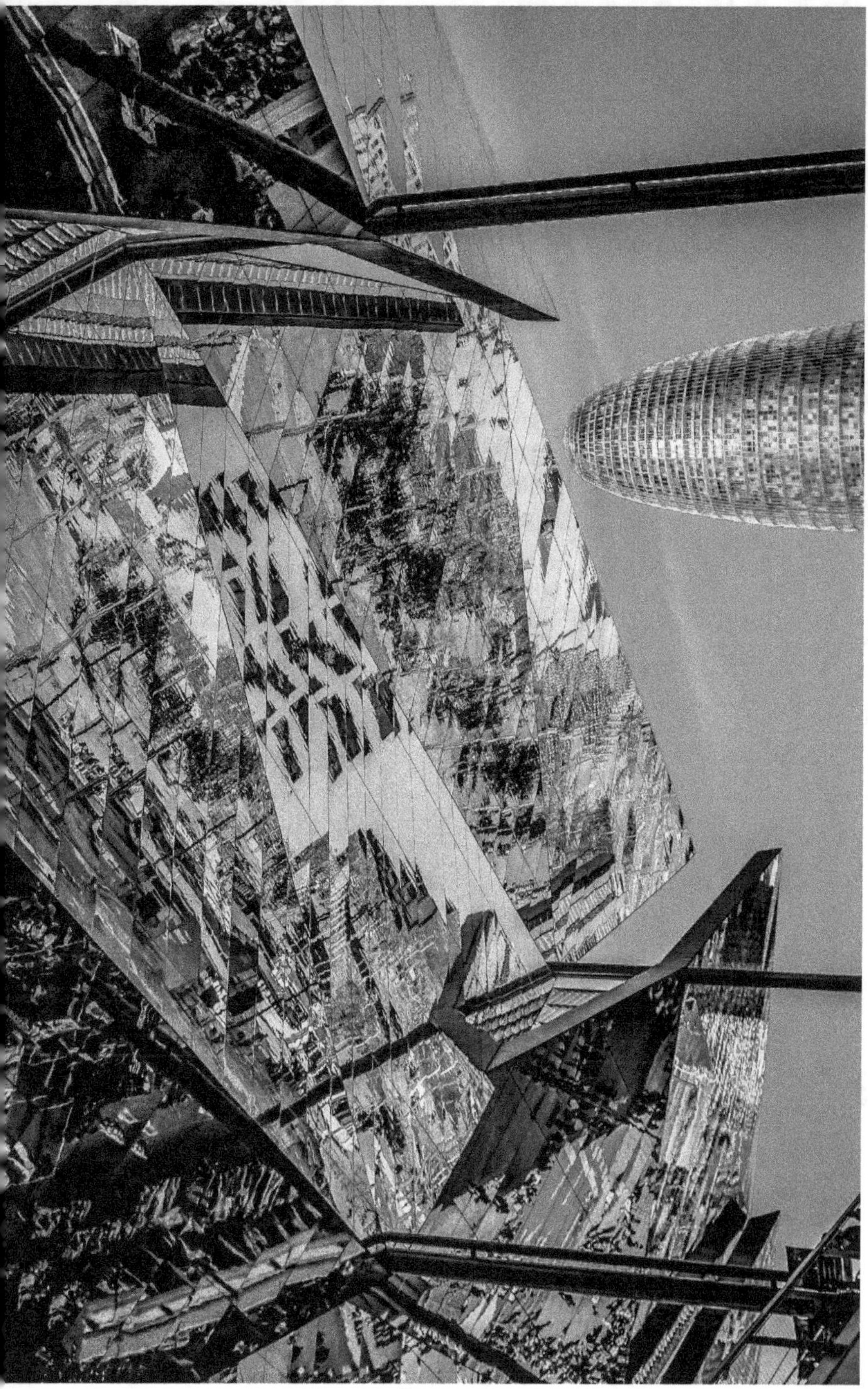

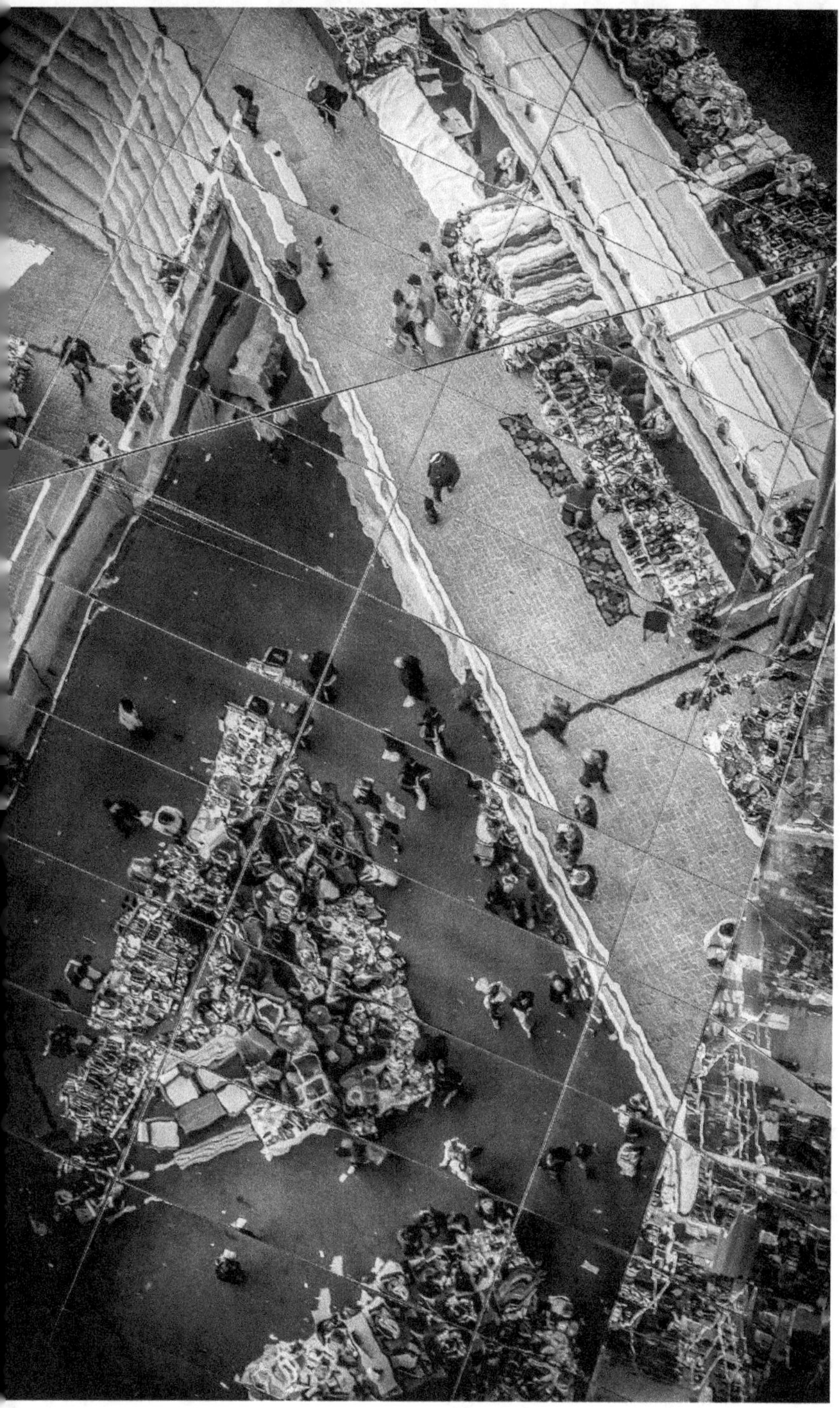

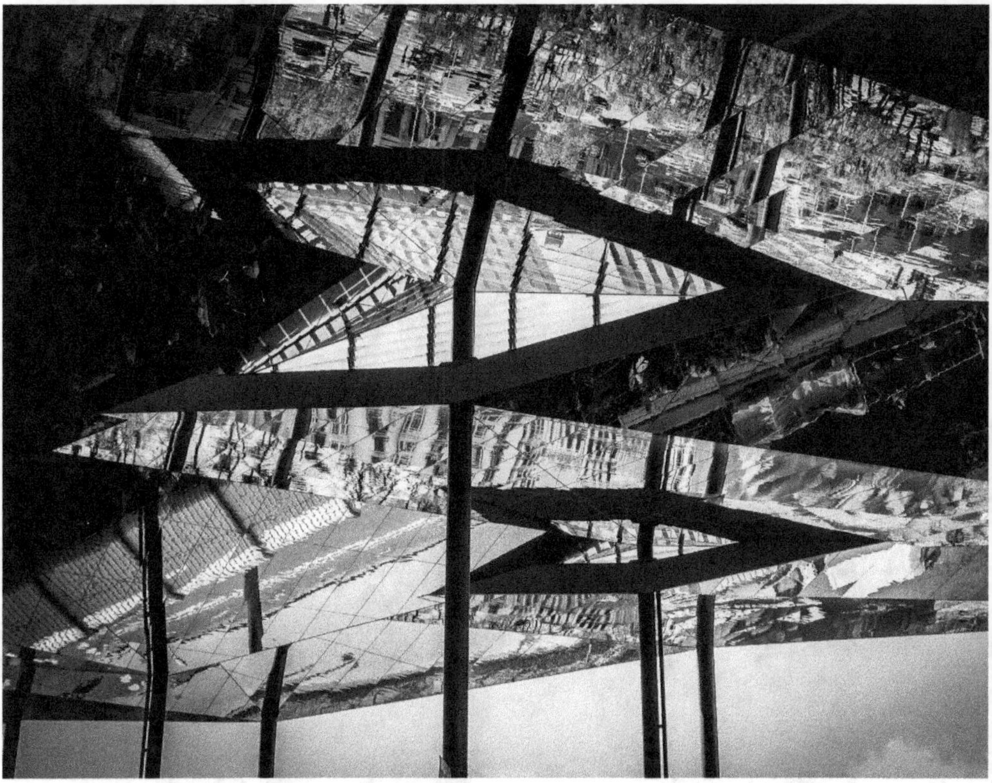

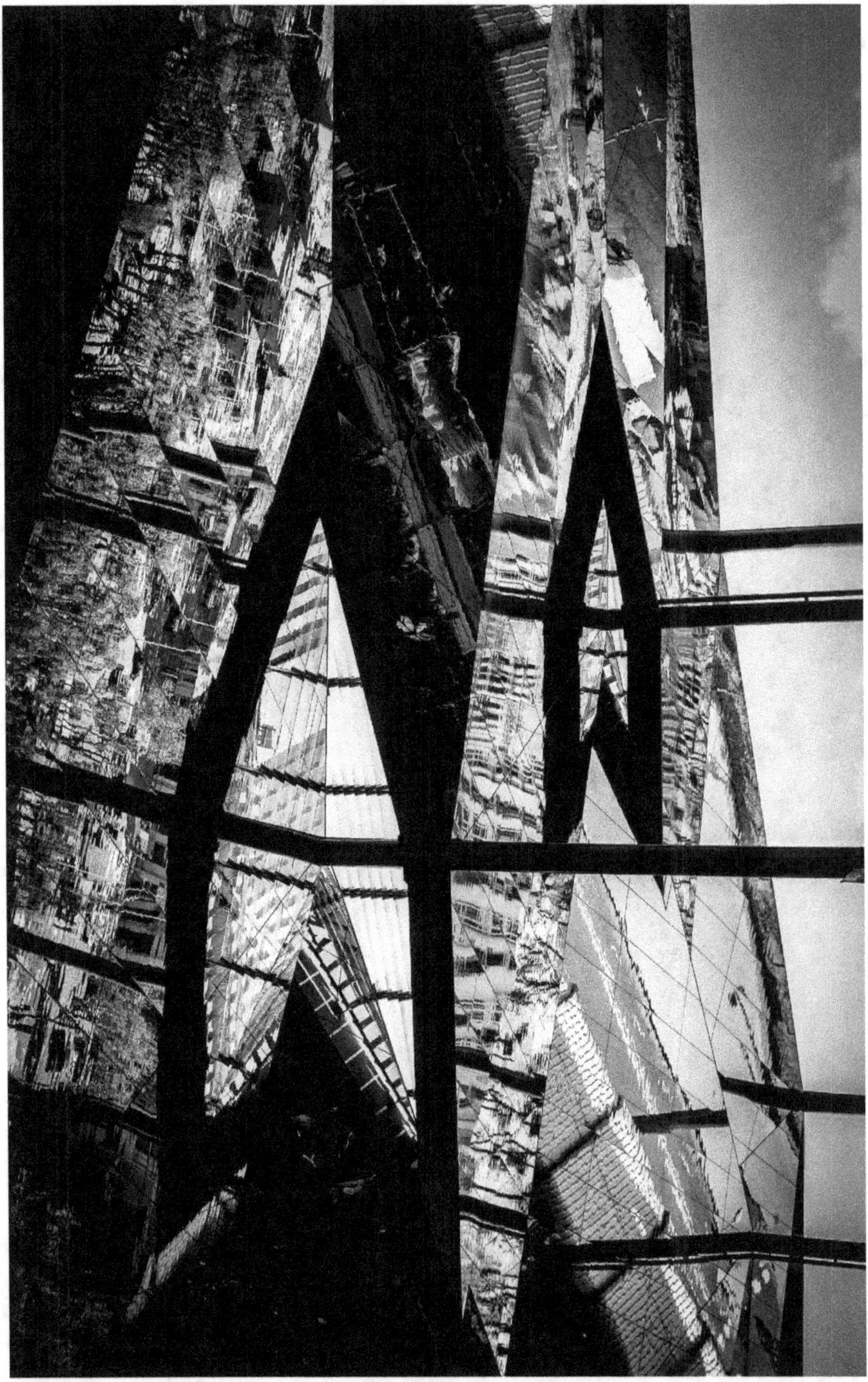

SECOND FLOOR

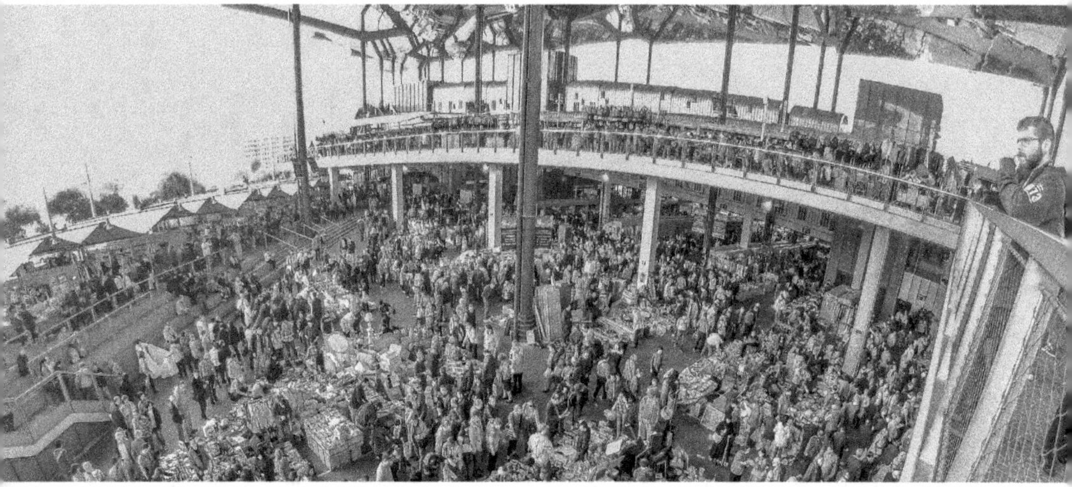

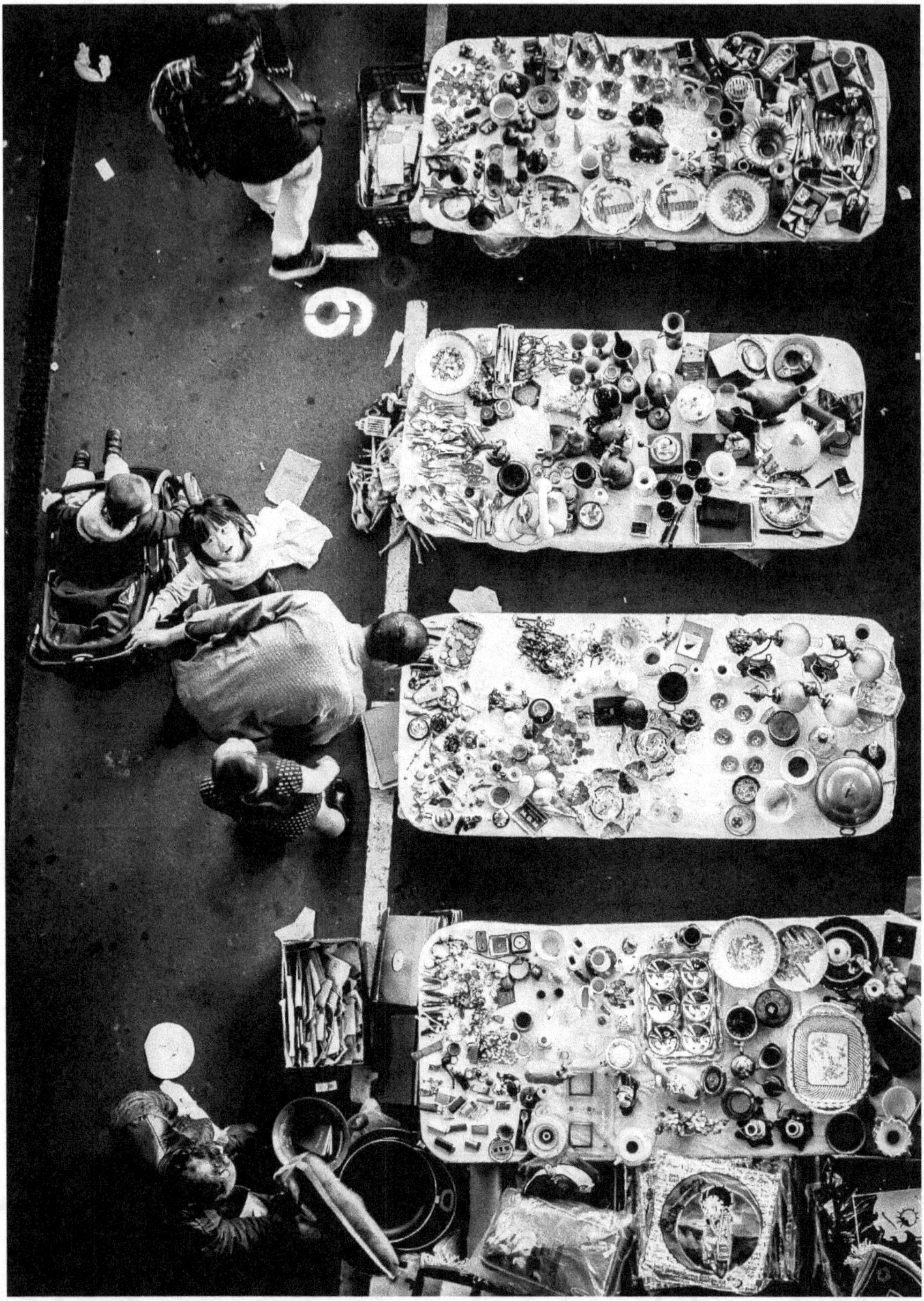

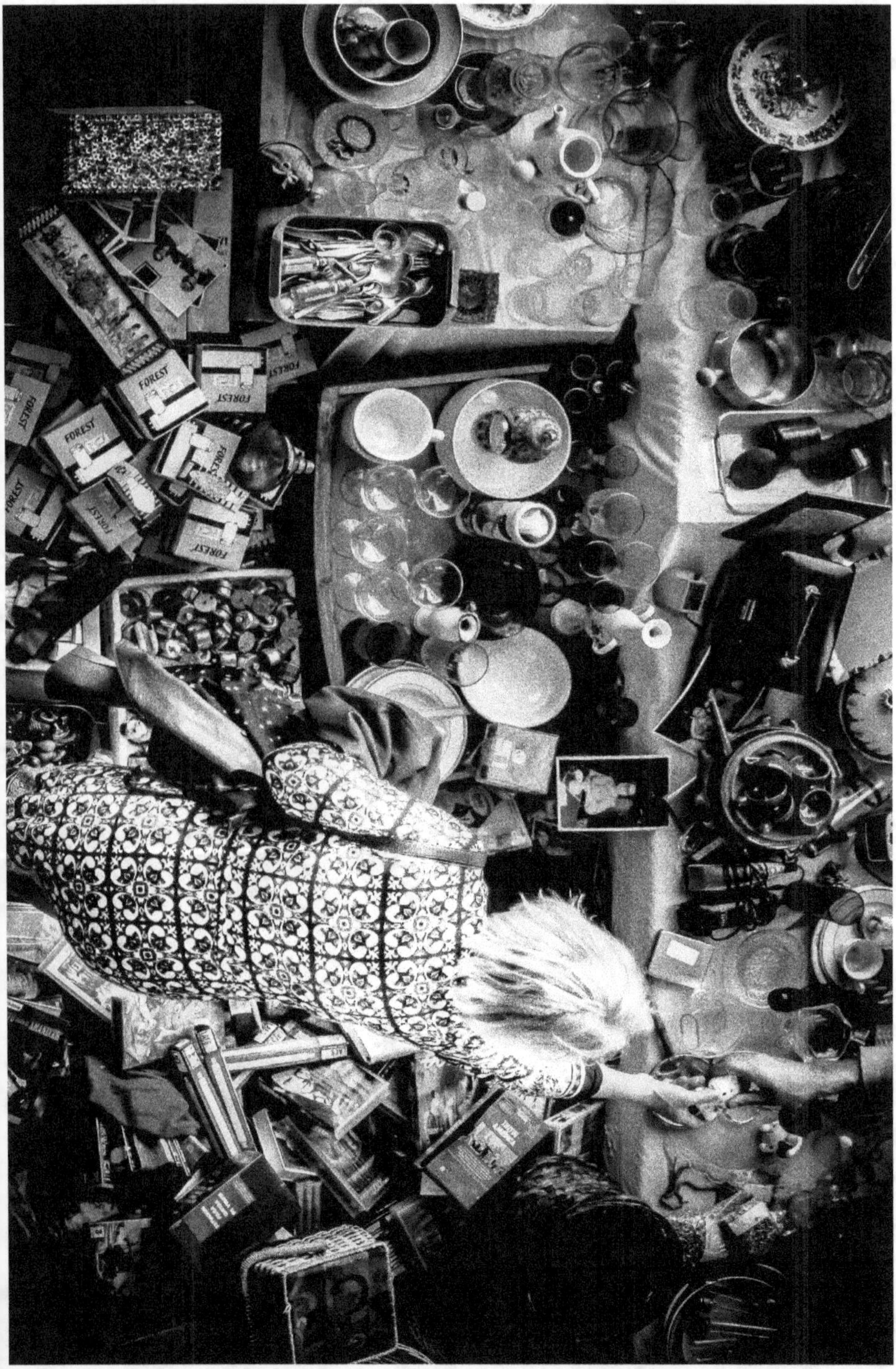
FOREST
FOREST
FOREST
FOREST
FOREST

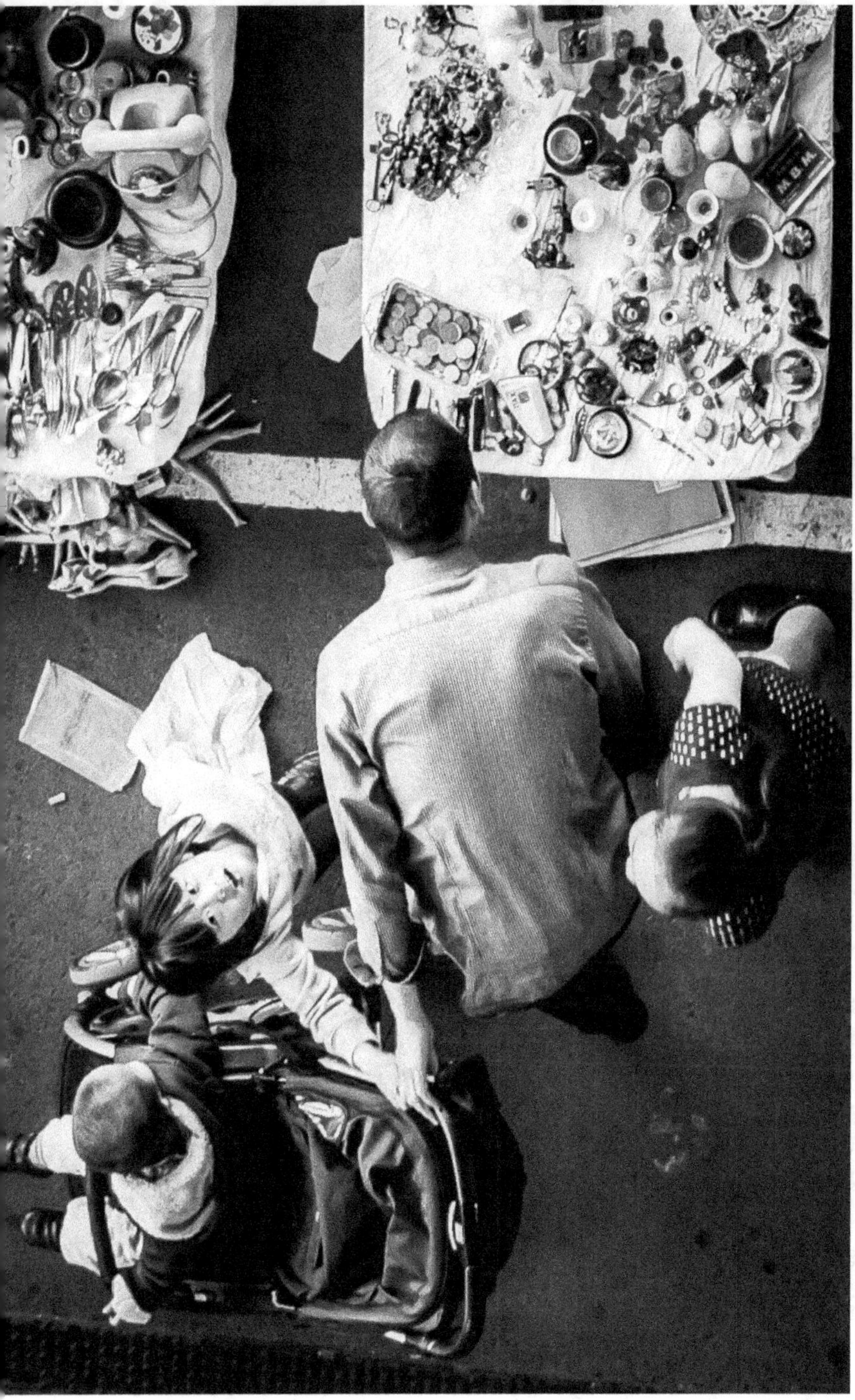

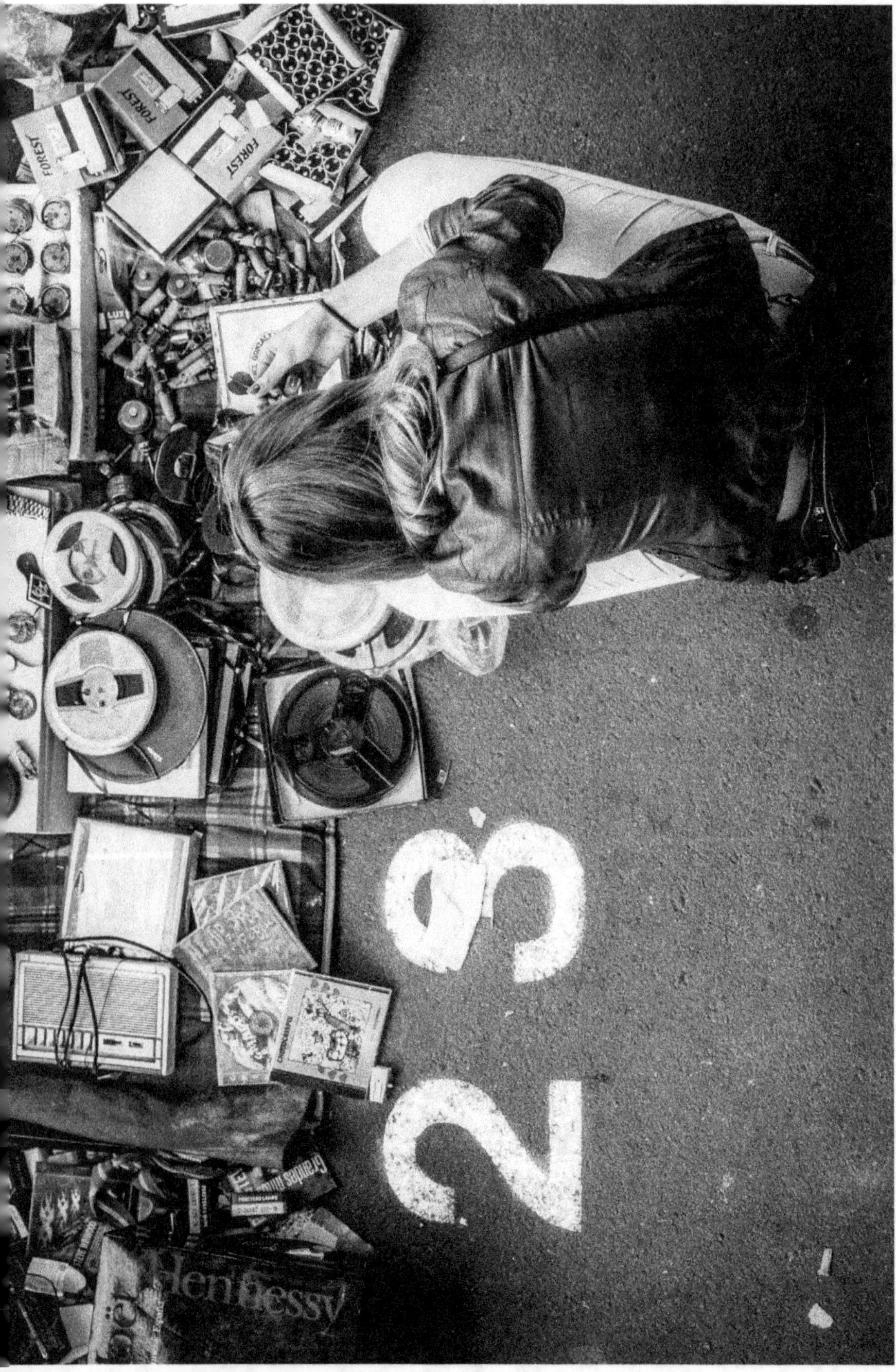
23
FOREST

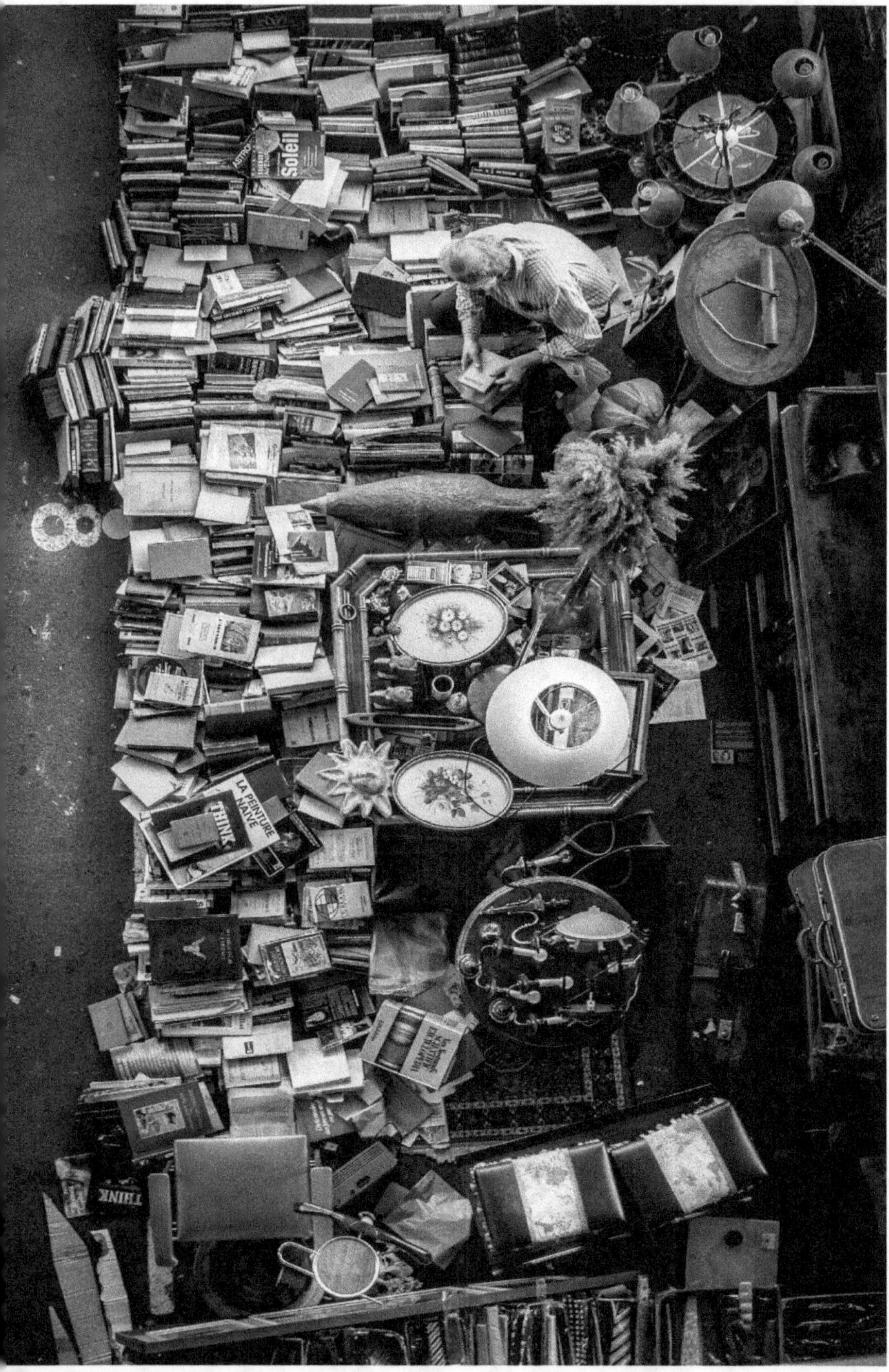
Soleil
LA PEINTURE NAIVE
THINK
THINK

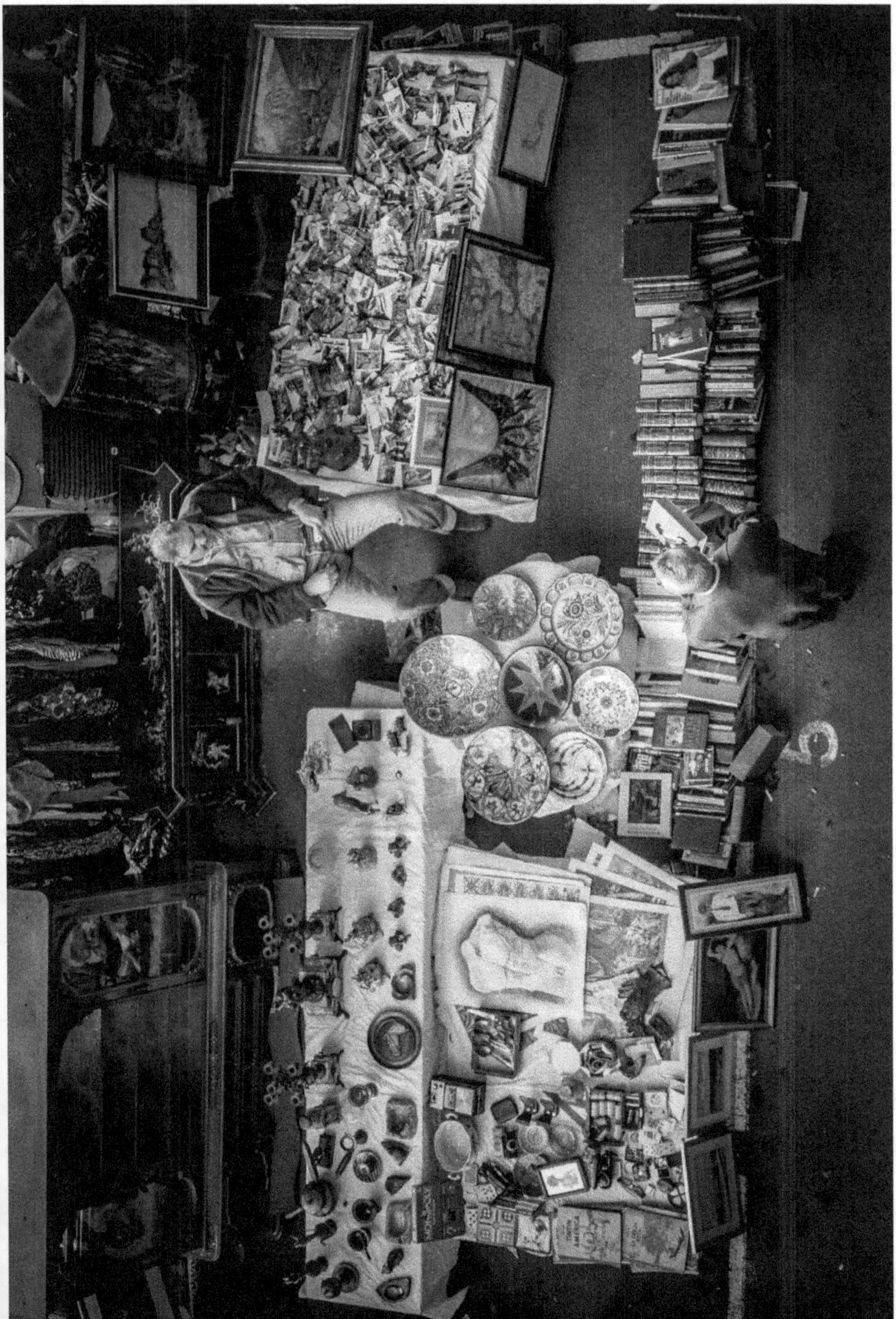

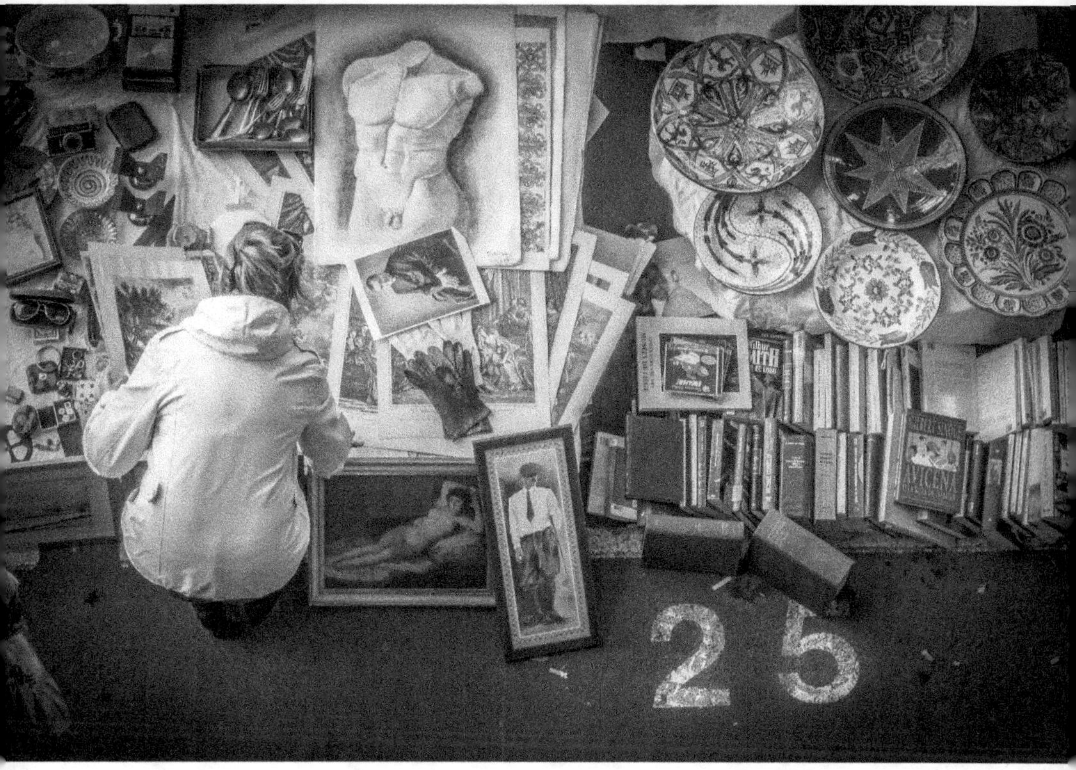
AVICENA
25

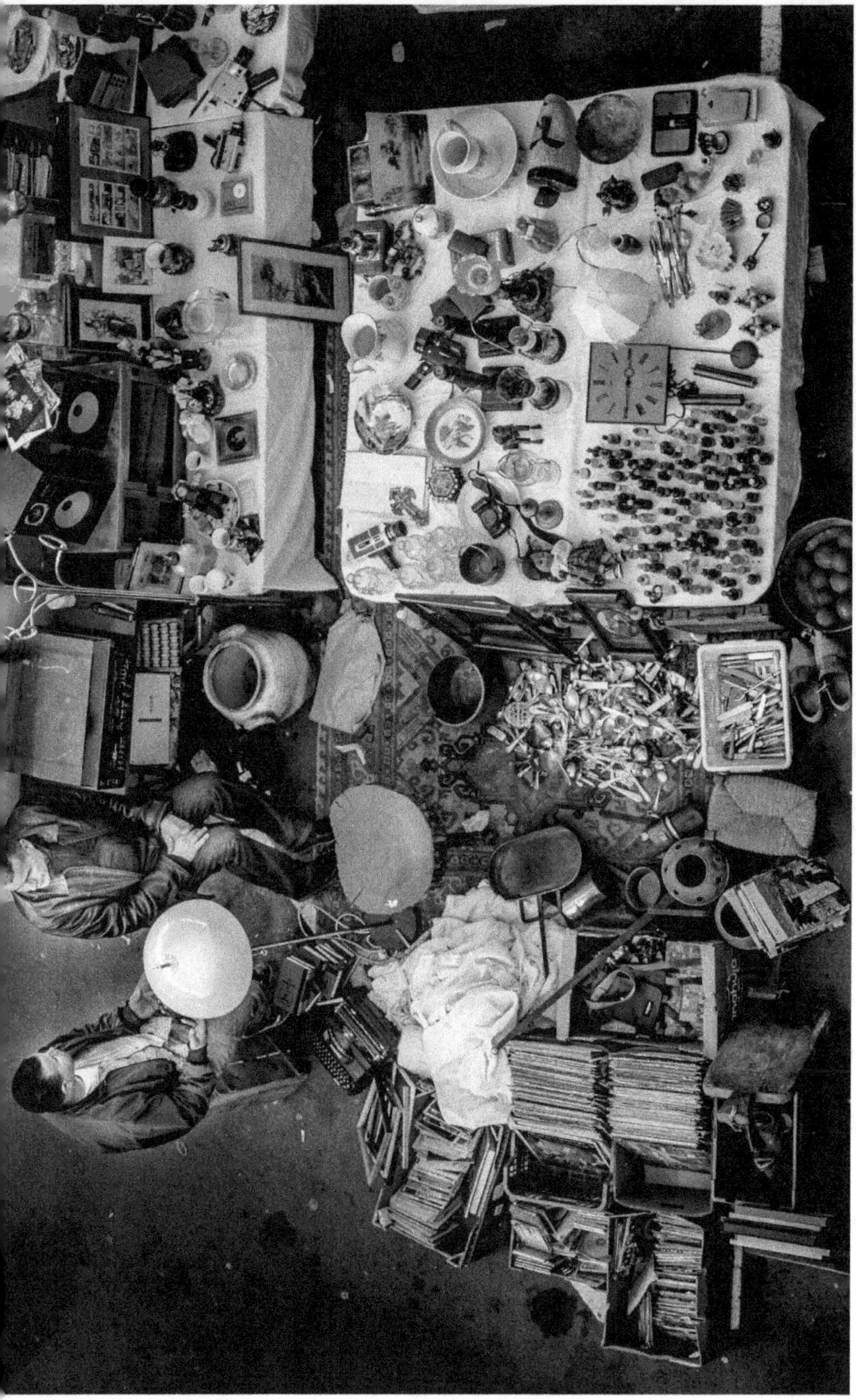

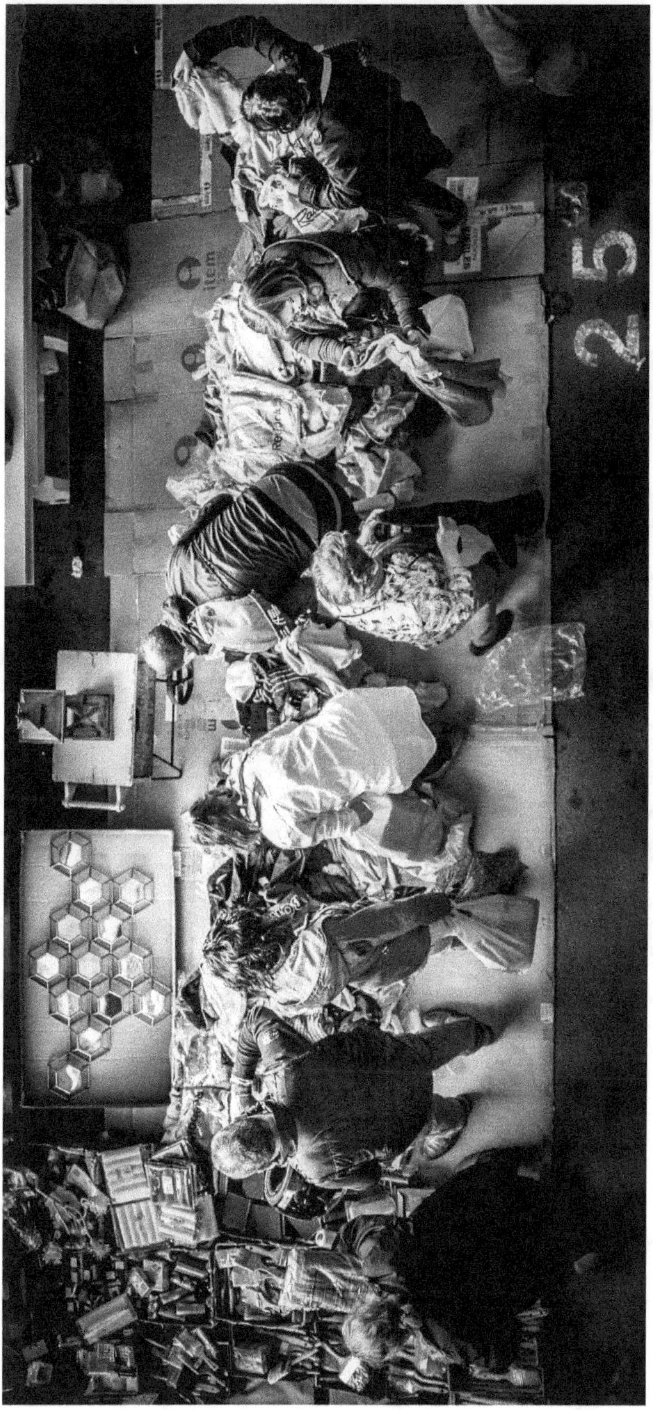
25

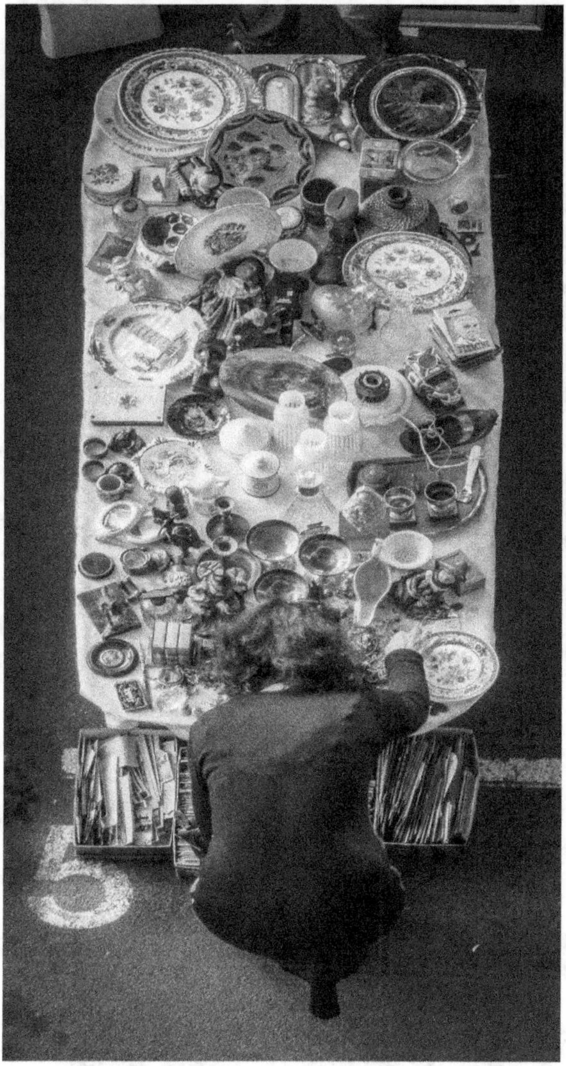

FIRST FLOOR

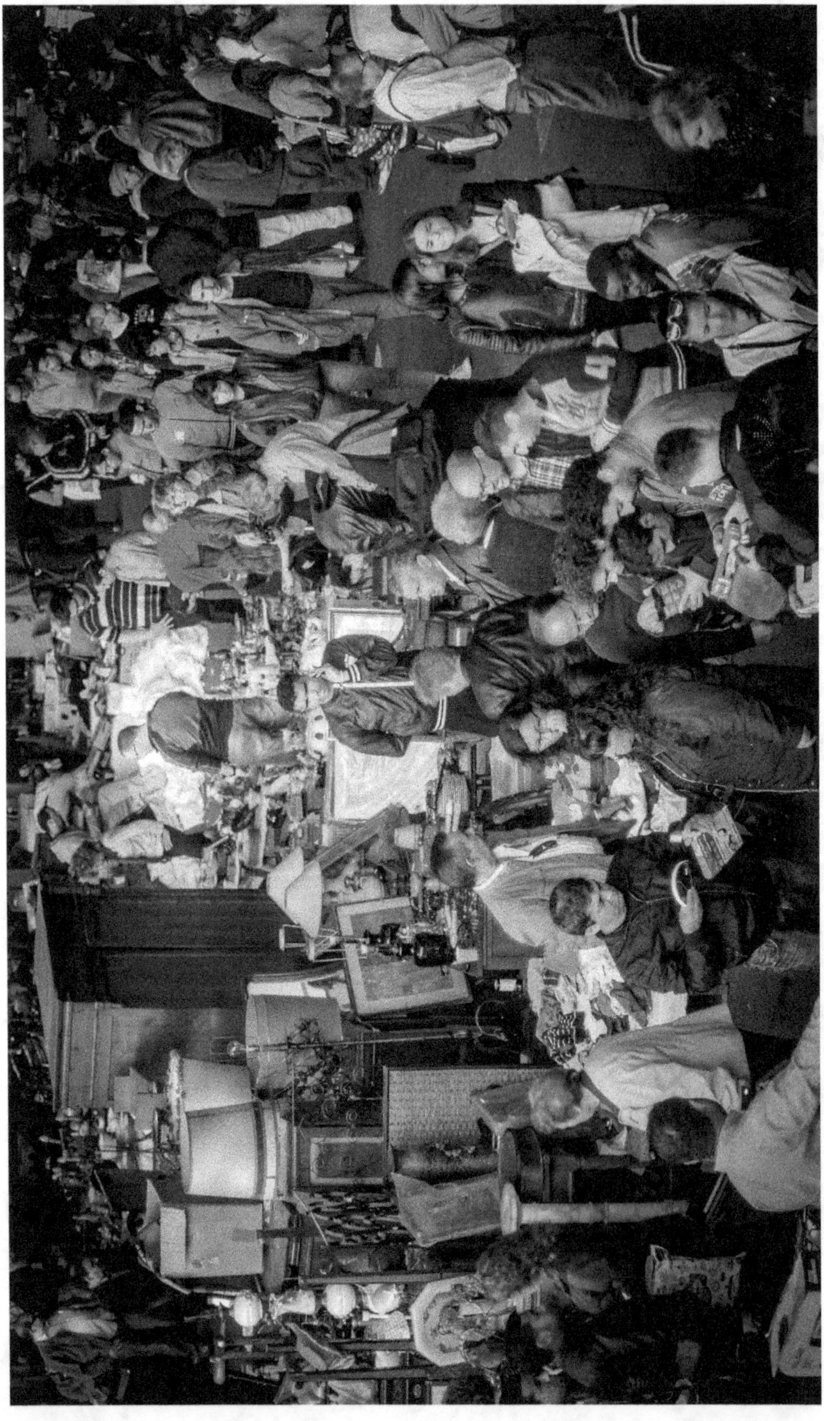

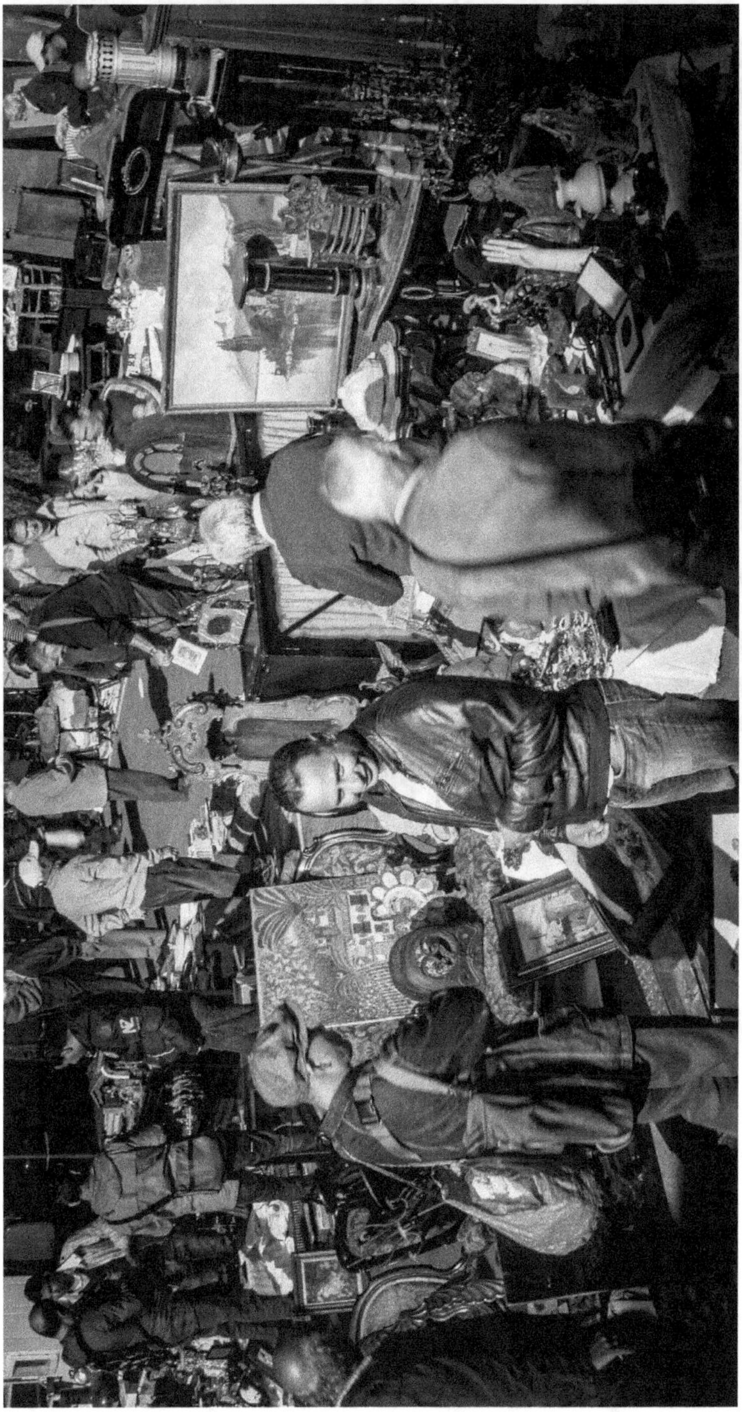

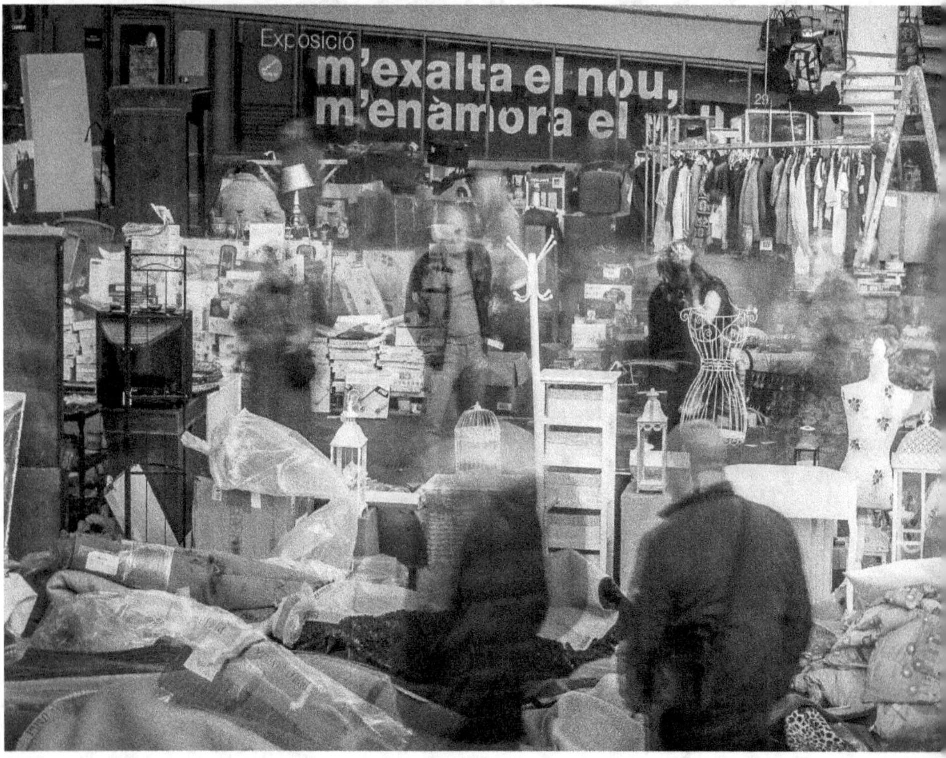
Exposició
m'exalta el nou,
m'enamora el

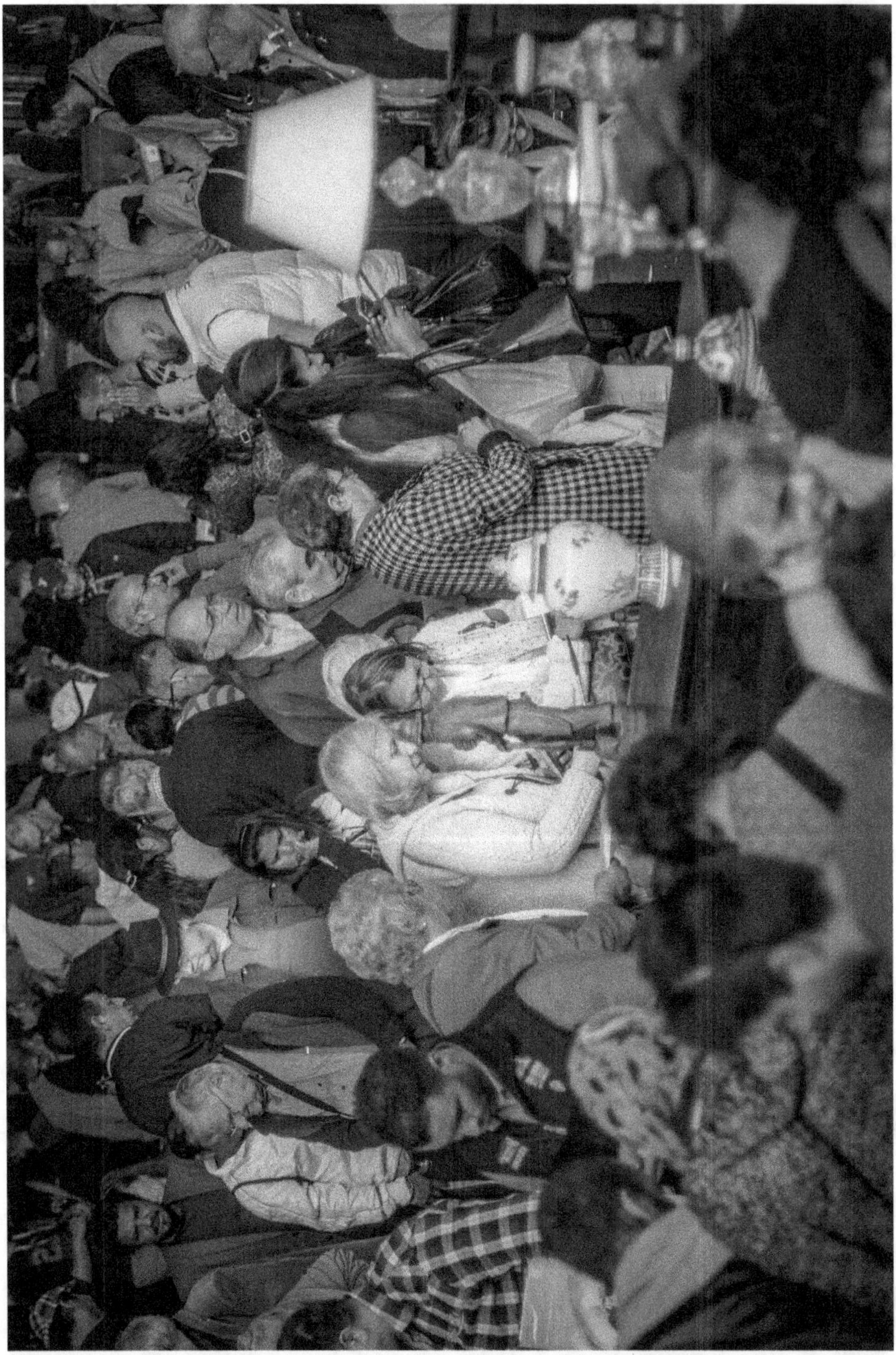

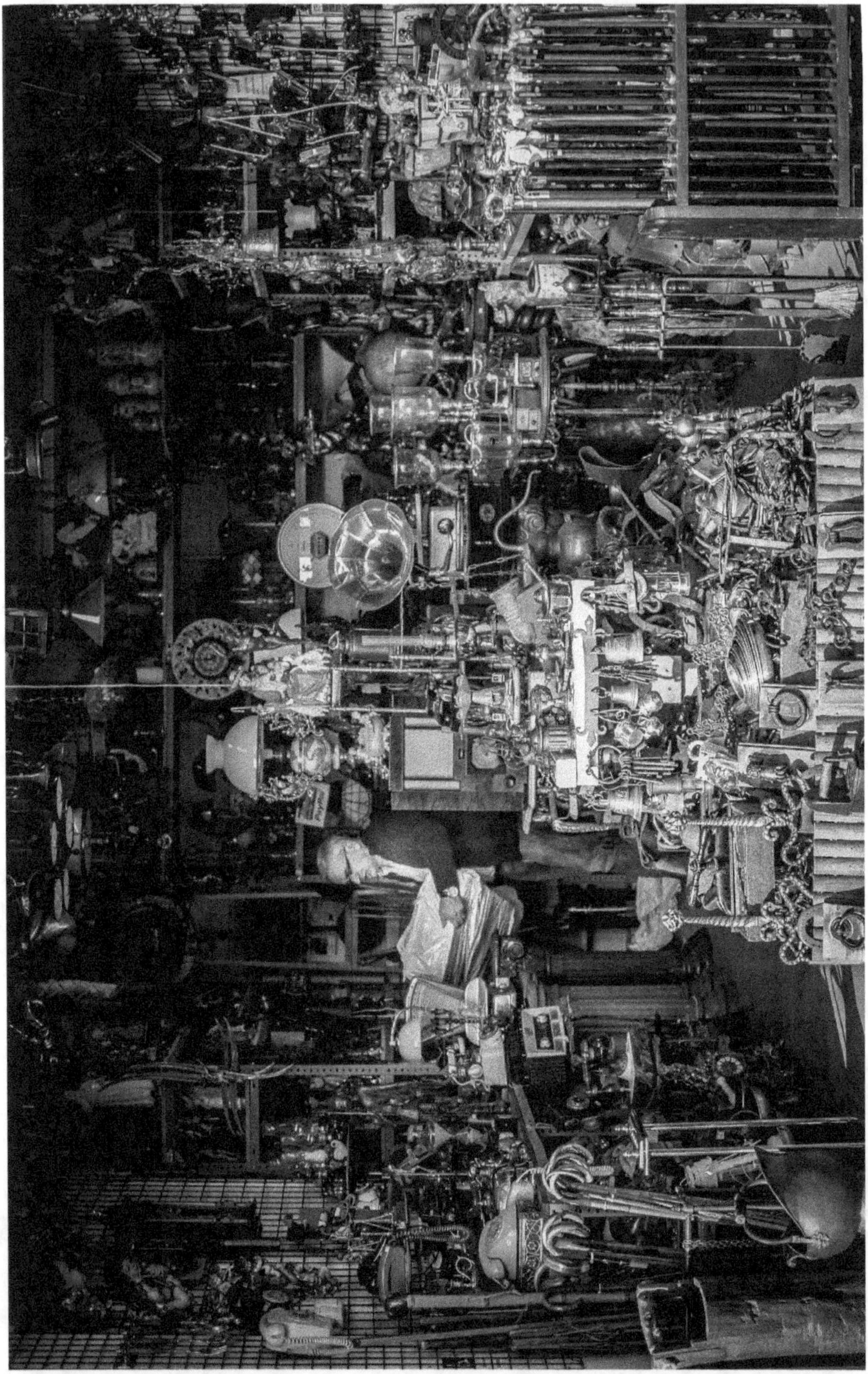

FLOOR

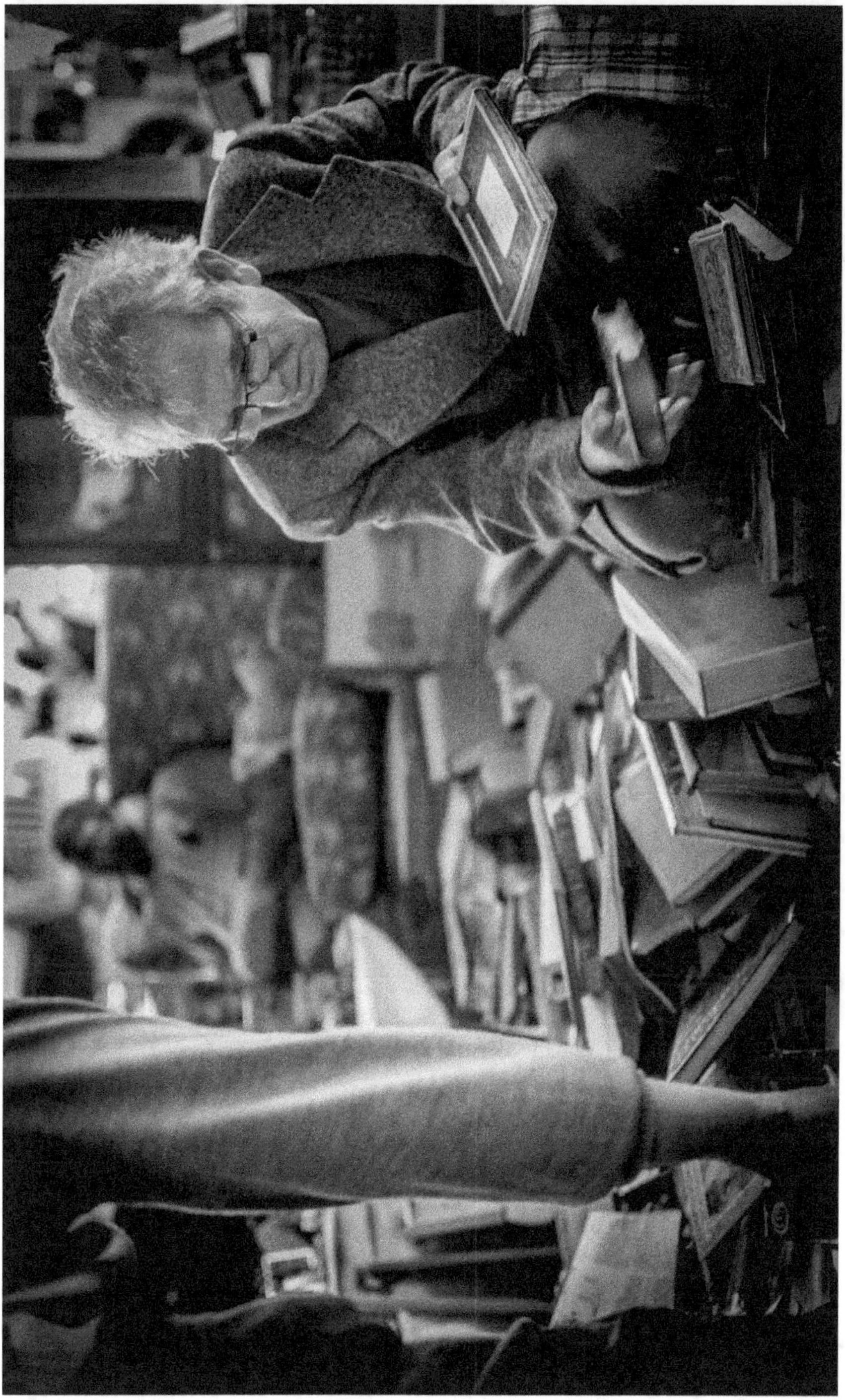

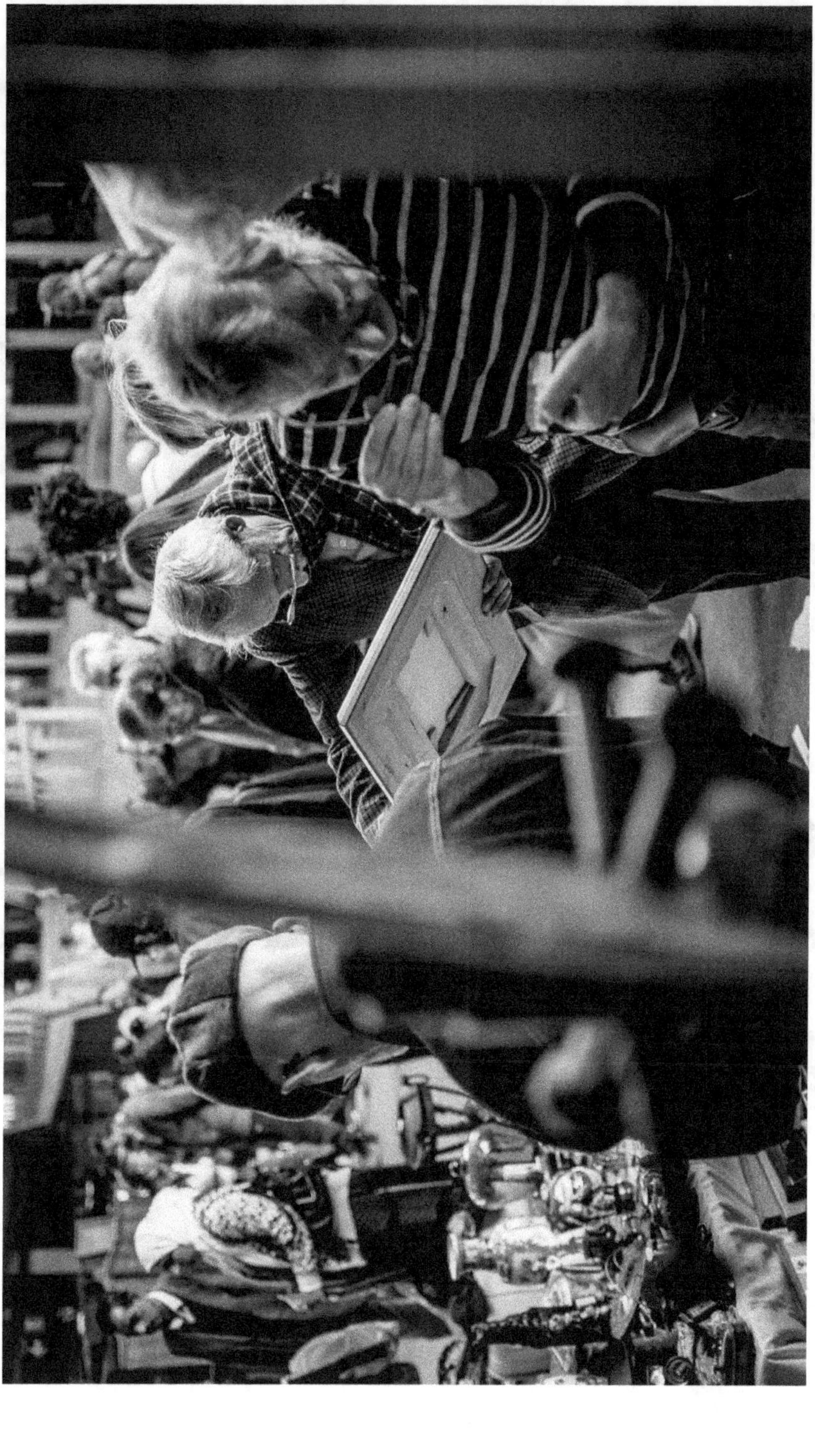

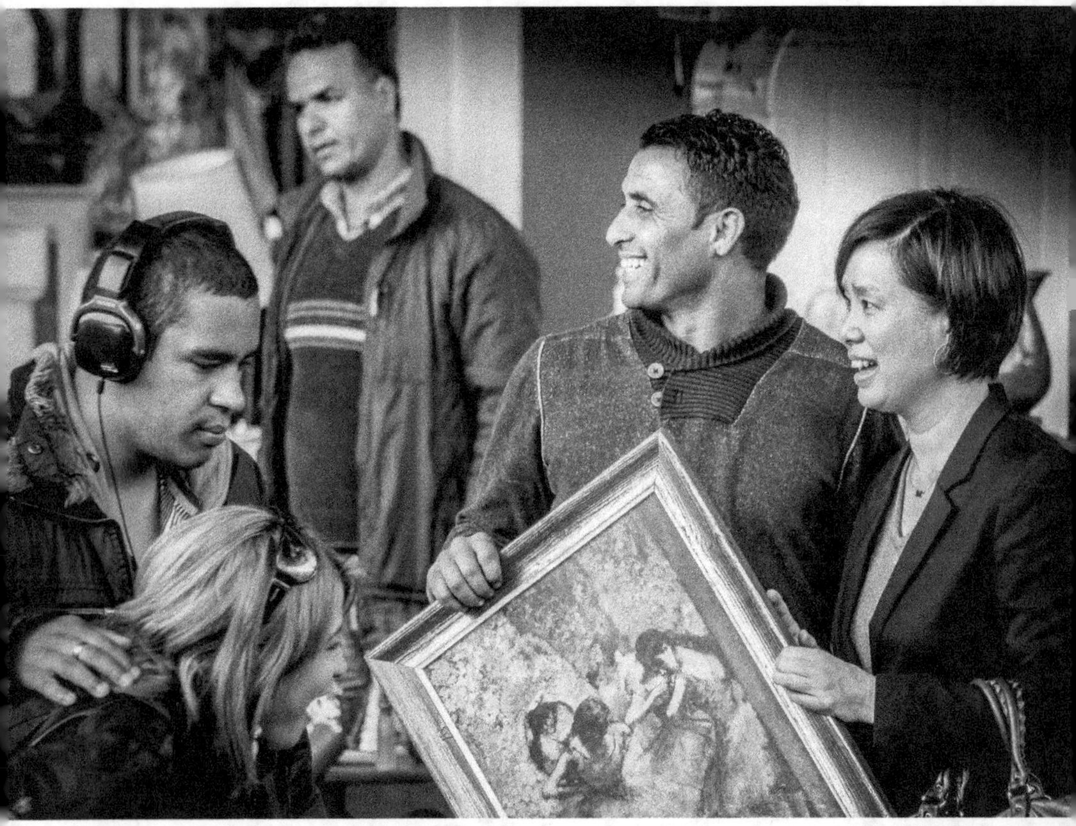

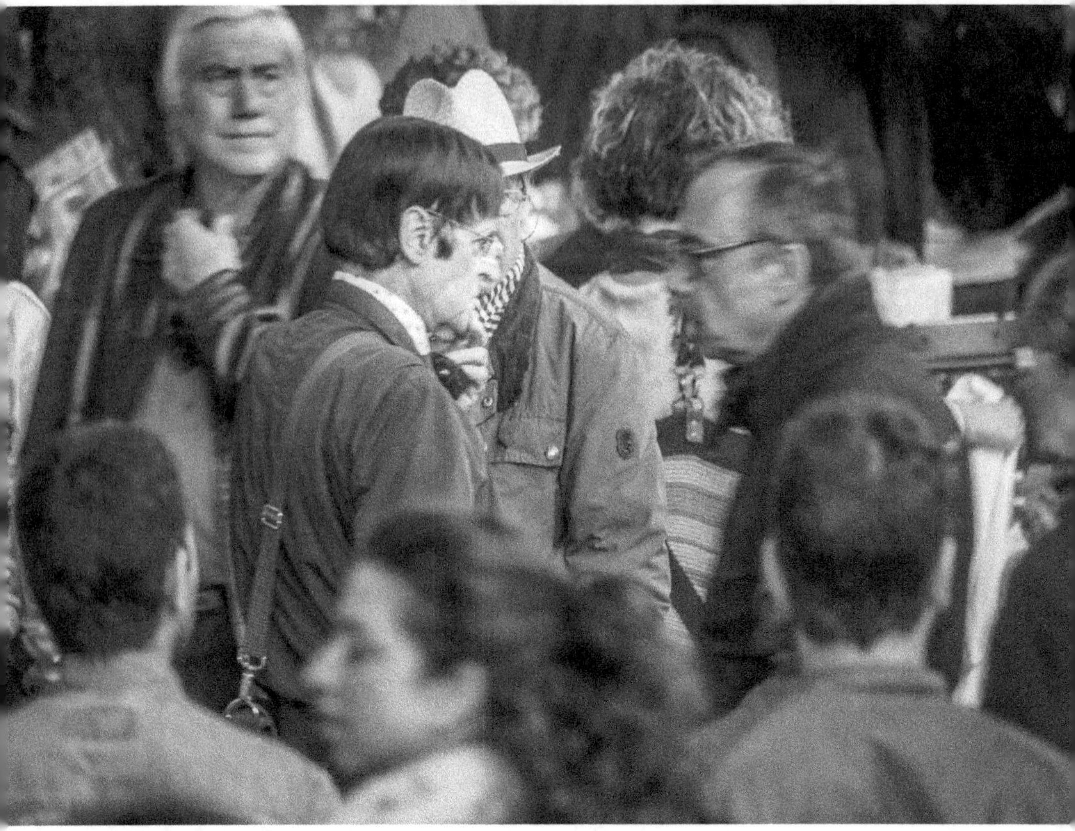

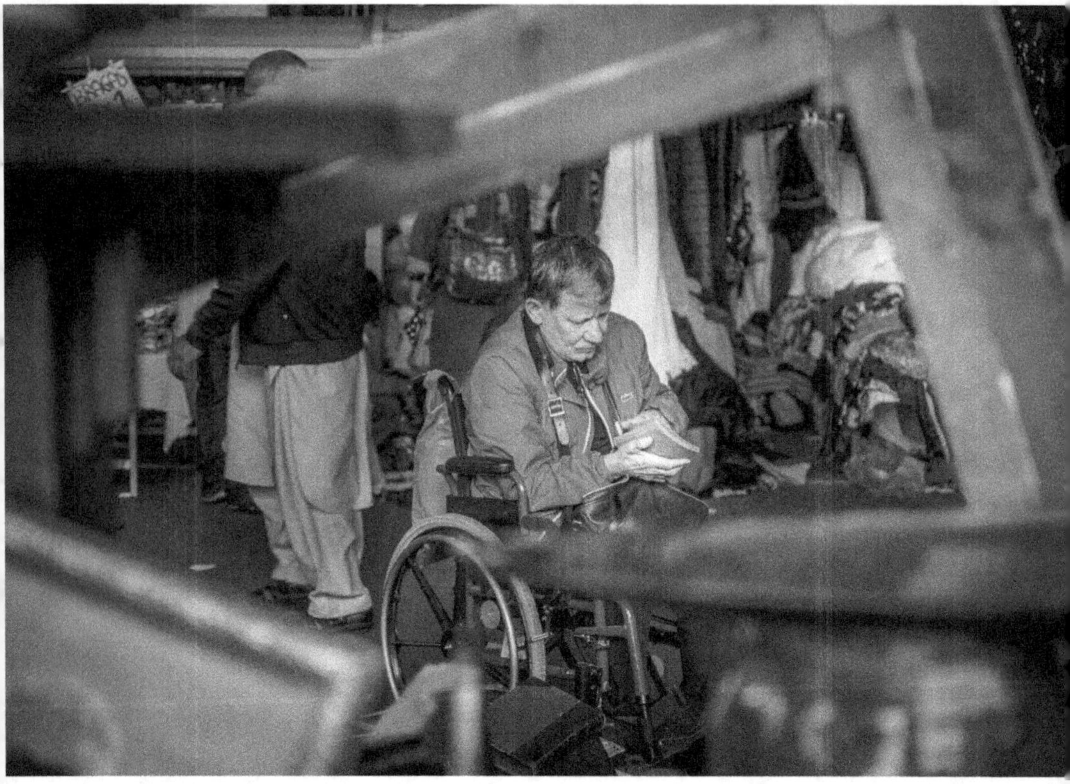

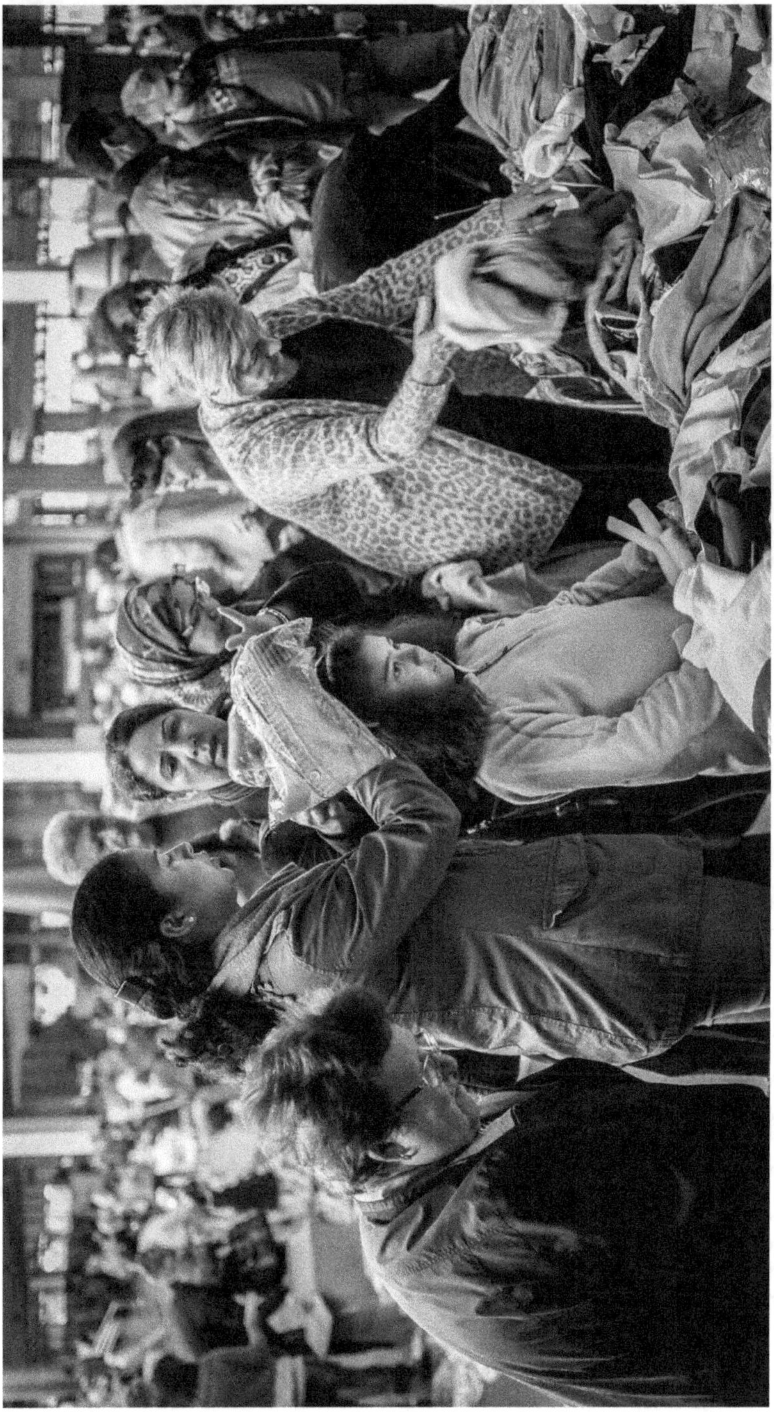

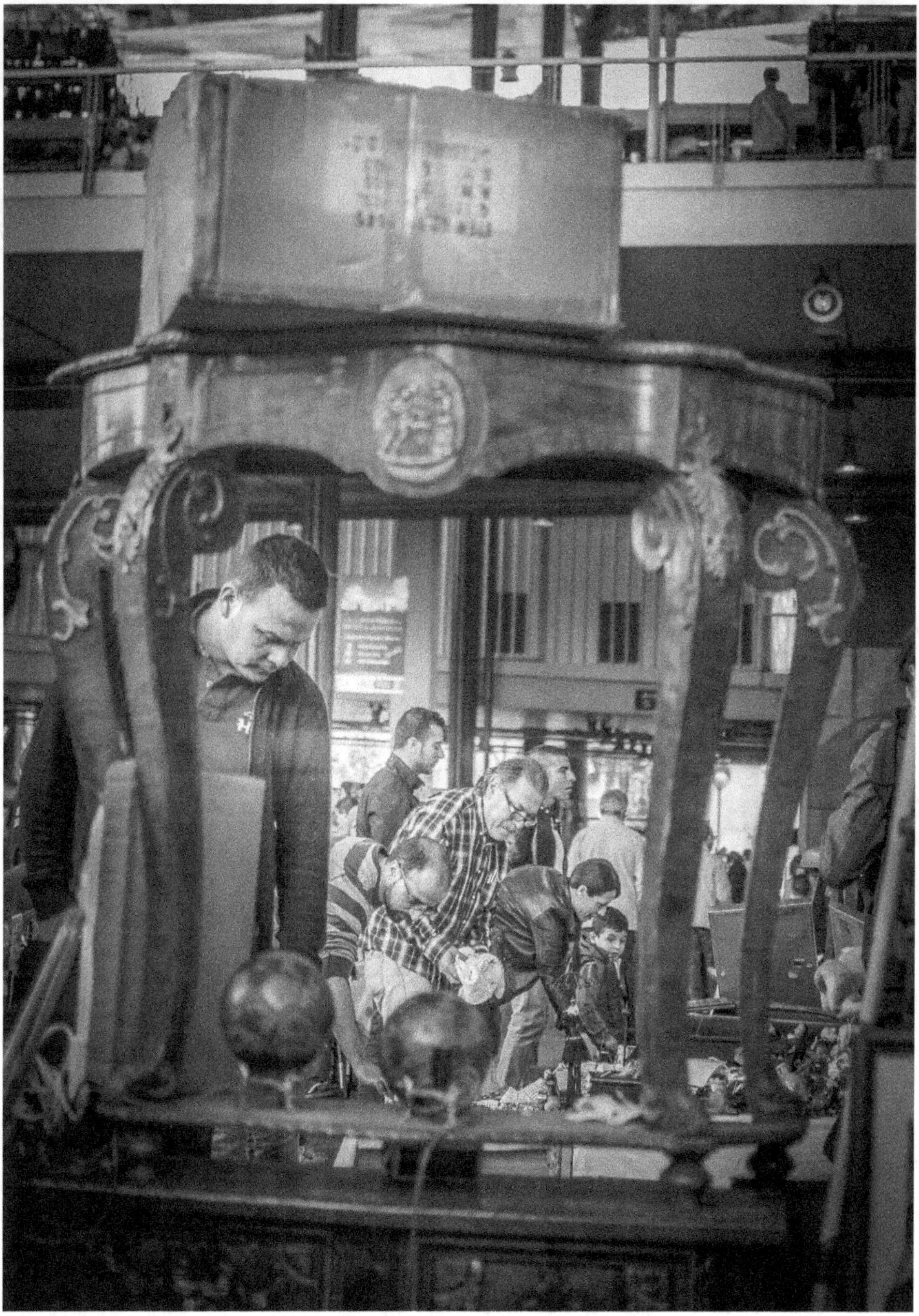

OBJECTS

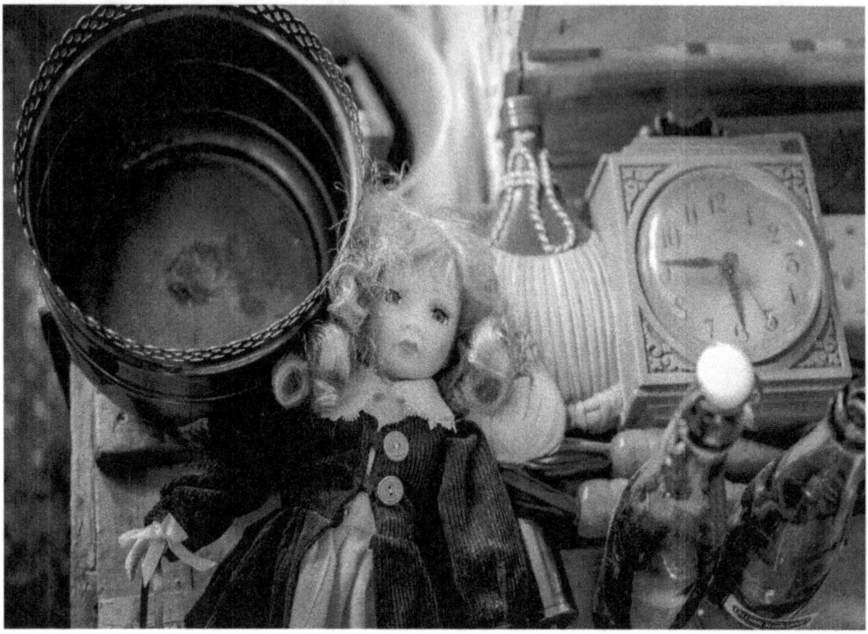

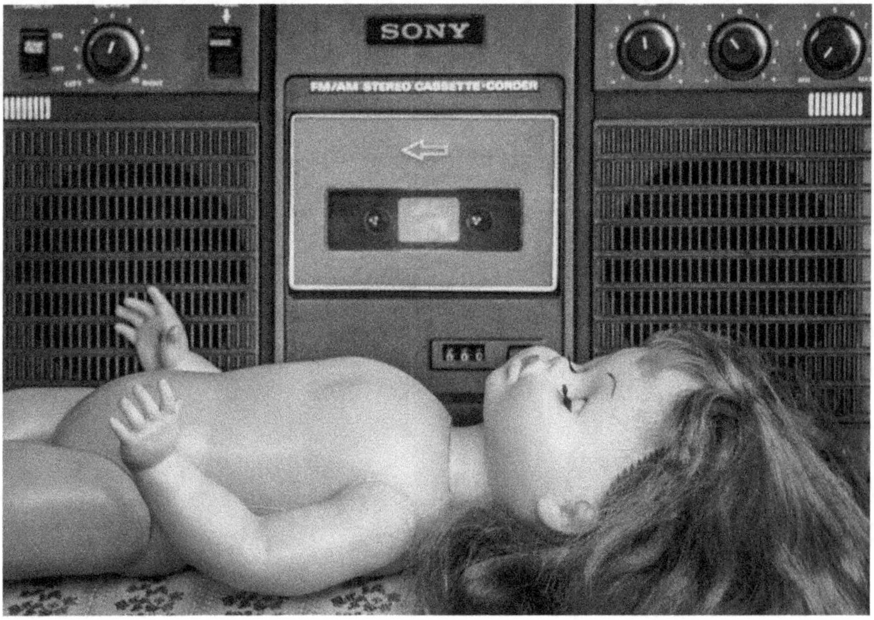
SONY
FM/AM STEREO CASSETTE-CORDER

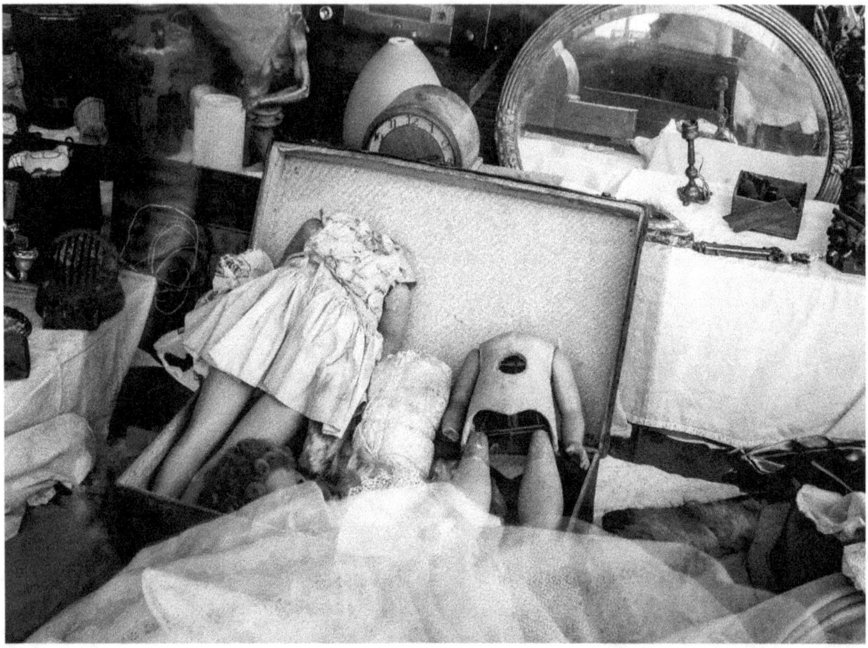

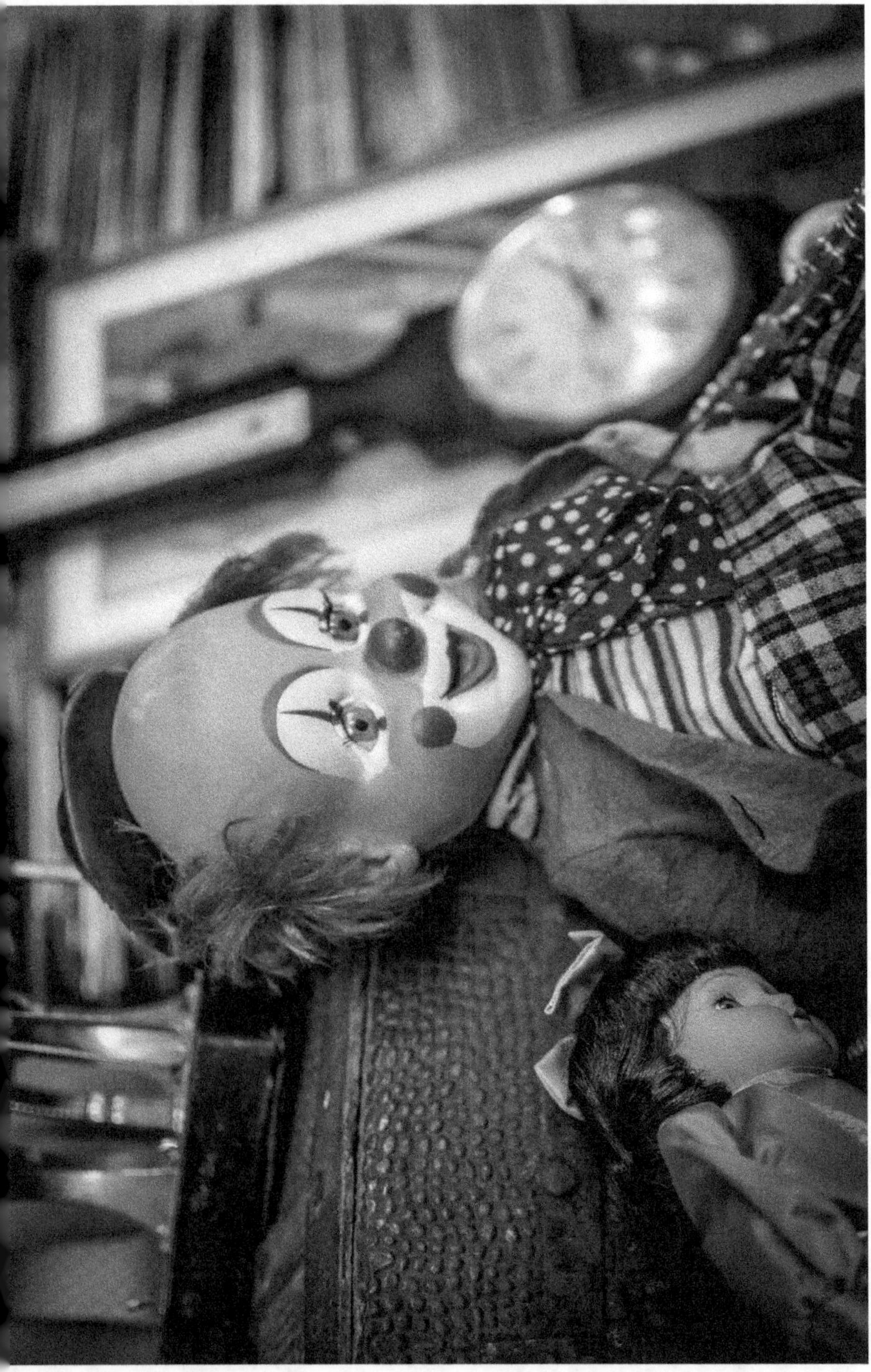

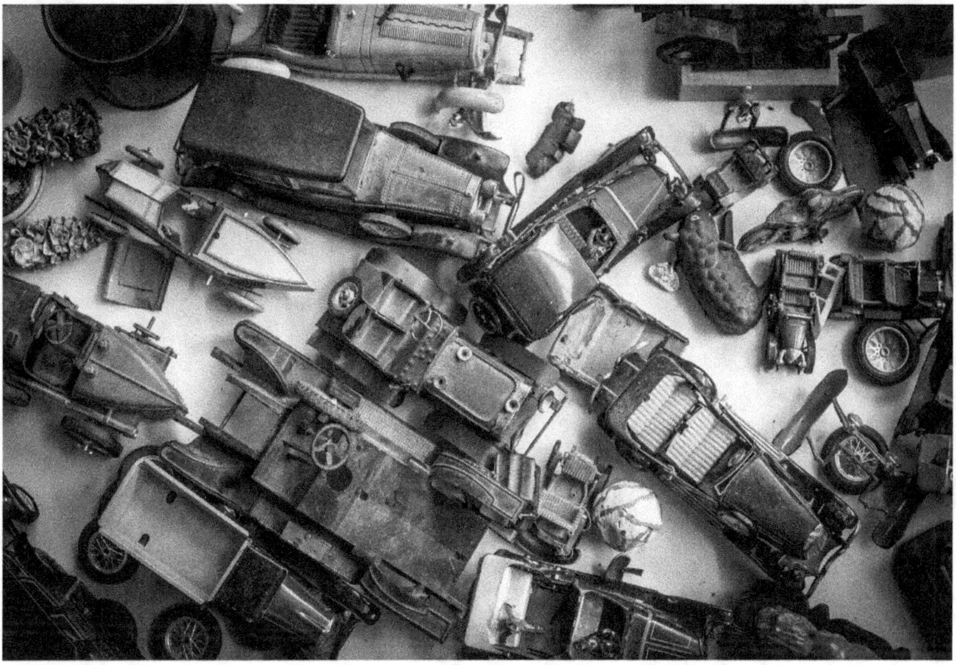

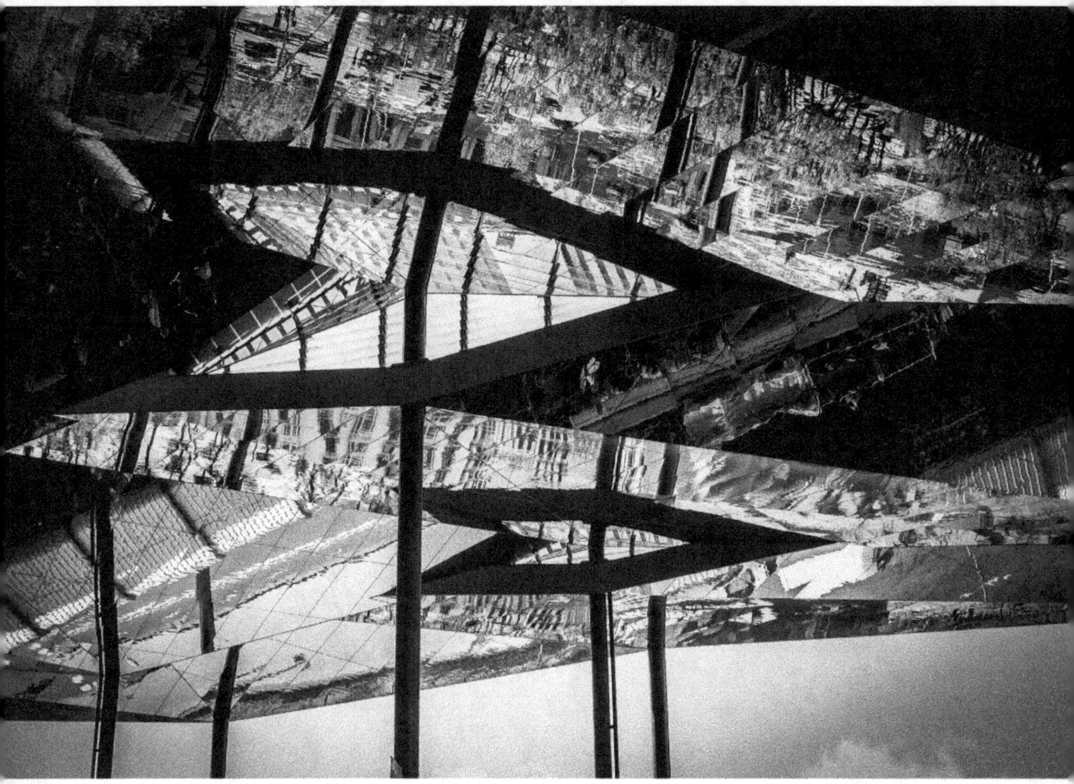

THE NEW BARCELONA

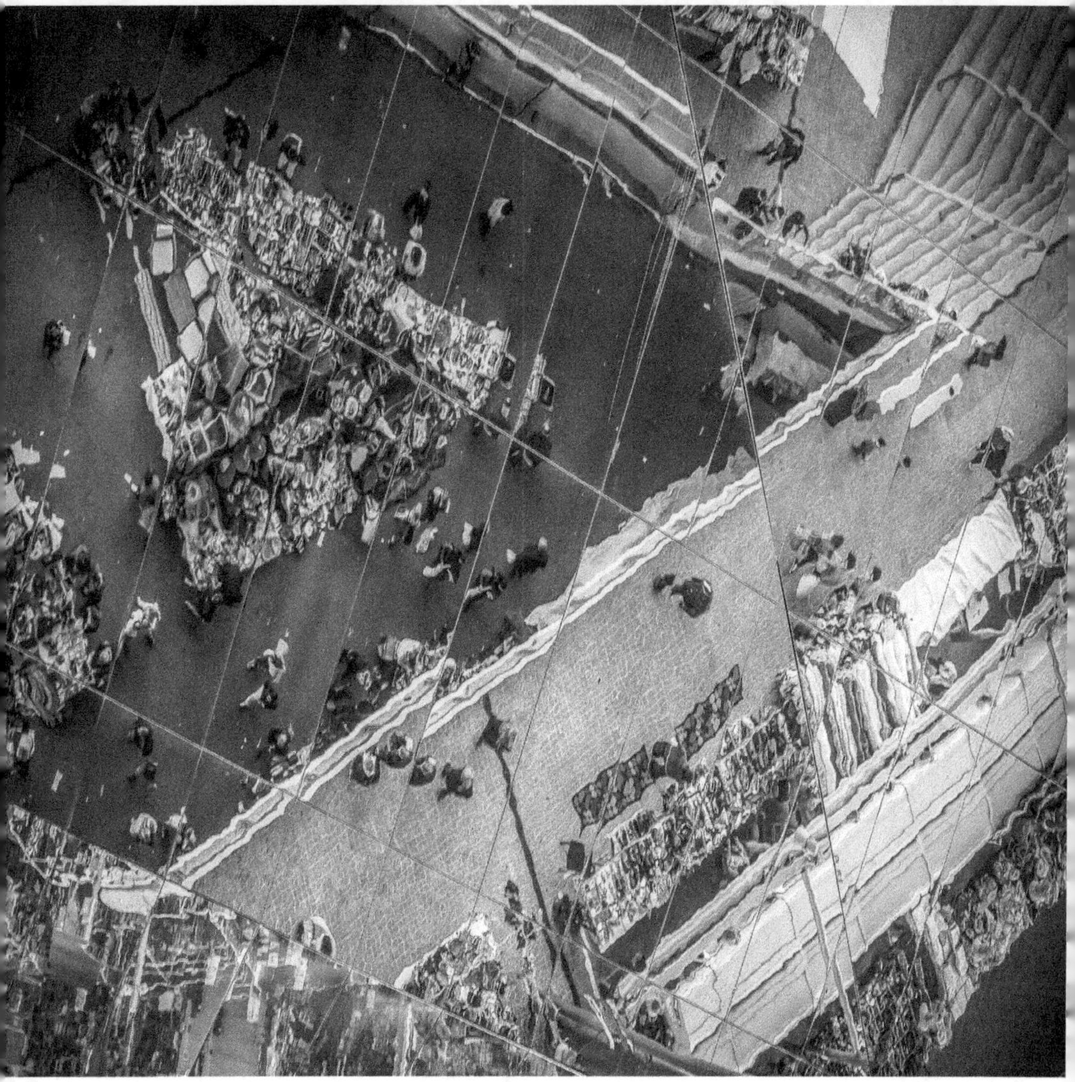

(OR NOT)